Drawing Cats

A STEP-BY-STEP GUIDE FOR ARTISTS

Drawing Cats

A STEP-BY-STEP GUIDE FOR ARTISTS

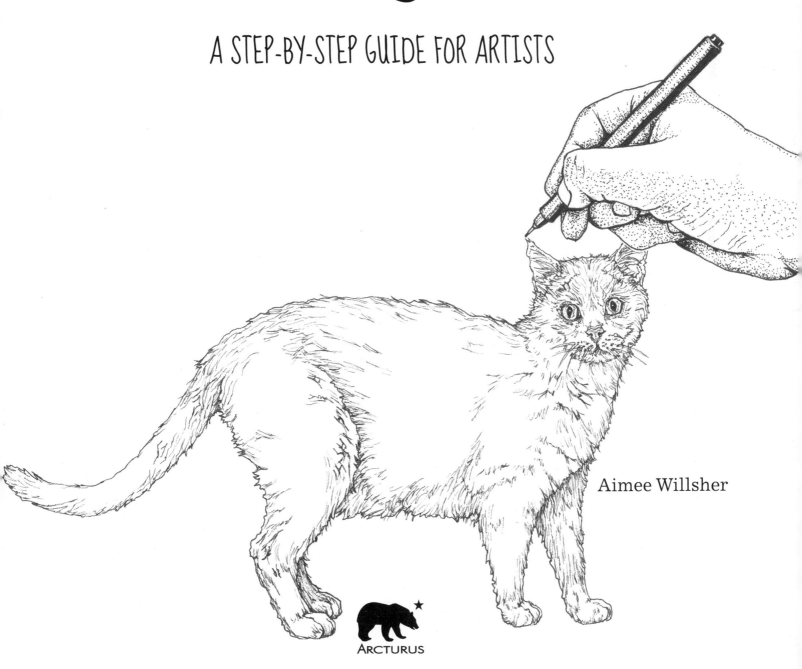

Aimee Willsher

ARCTURUS

ARCTURUS

This edition published in 2016
by Arcturus Publishing Limited
26/27 Bickels Yard,
151–153 Bermondsey Street,
London SE1 3HA

ISBN: 978-1-78404-744-3
AD004585UK

Printed in China

CONTENTS

Introduction

Cats are among the world's most popular pets, as they are easy-going, independent creatures; they love to be out and about but always return for some love and attention from their owner. No two cats are the same and no one cat will be the same from one day to the next! Even if you don't have a cat of your own, just take a walk down any residential street and you are bound to encounter one sooner or later; some of your friends probably have cats, too. This easy availability makes cats excellent subject matter for any budding artist who wants to develop their drawing skills.

There are many breeds of cat, offering a diversity of physical characteristics with which to experiment and develop your style and technique.

We shall start by looking at some basic anatomy and how the form of the cat can be broken down into the simple shapes that everyone will be familiar with. We shall then look at how to combine these shapes to create the more complex outline of the cat and finally learn visual tricks to add flesh and texture to the outline and capture the illusion of a three-dimensional form upon the flat piece of paper.

After the basics have been covered you will be guided through drawing projects, from easy to more challenging, using step-by-step examples which demonstrate how to build up a simple outline into a beautifully detailed composition. By following this method, at the end of your journey through this book you will be able to immortalize cats in beautiful works of art that can be treasured forever.

GETTING STARTED

You don't need to splash out on a lot of expensive materials before you start your artistic adventures; a pencil and a few blank sheets of paper are all you need to begin. Making a first mark on pristine paper can be daunting, but don't let the possibility of making a mistake unsettle you. Learning to draw is just like attempting to acquire any new skill; your first attempts may not be perfect but with a little practice and determination you will soon see how your techniques become increasingly sophisticated.

The first exercises in the book may seem a little mundane, but by getting these simple techniques under your belt at an early stage you will be able to tackle more complex images very quickly and with relative ease. You will soon be making beautiful drawings that any artist would be proud of!

Basic materials and accessories

The enormous variety of materials and brands to be found in art supplies stores on the street and online can be daunting, but as you have already learnt, all you need is a few basics to begin with. As you continue your exploration of drawing techniques you will be able to decide for yourself the types and brands of materials that work best for you. Most essential materials for drawing are relatively inexpensive, so there is plenty of room for experimentation.

PAPER

To start with, all you'll need is a standard sketch pad from your local stationery shop. As you move on to experimenting with different materials, though, it's a good idea to use a specialized paper which will provide a surface designed to get the best out of a particular medium. Paper is graded according to its weight, and this is usually displayed on the front of a sketch pad – the higher the number, the thicker the paper. Paper graded as 120 gsm (75 lb) is quite thin, fairly cheap and great for making quick practice sketches. As the weight of the paper increases, so does the price; a thick 300 gsm (140 lb) paper is perfect for working on more developed, detailed drawings. Its thickness means it can withstand blending, watercolour washes and heavy shading without tearing or curling.

Another factor to consider is the surface. Paper with a texture or 'grain' is great when you start experimenting with charcoal and pastel since the nature of the surface gives the medium something to engage with.

PENCILS

The trusty pencil is a tool that everyone will have used since early childhood. Pencils are a perfect medium with which to start, as they are hugely versatile – great for making quick sketches as well as more detailed, ambitious drawings.

Pencils are graded according to the density of their leads, from very soft to very hard. The grade is shown on the side of the pencil by means of a letter (or letter and number). Hard leads are graded as H to 9H, with 9H being the hardest; soft pencils are B to 9B (the softest). The HB pencil with which we are all familiar falls in the middle of this density scale.

Hard pencils are good for making fine, light lines; softer pencils are for creating dark lines. They are easily blended and can be used to build up smooth gradated shading. I tend not to use really hard pencils for drawing, because the lines they produce are too light to be easily visible. It's a good idea to buy a tin of pencils containing a range of leads which will cater for all your needs when you are starting to discover the results you can obtain from different grades of pencil.

WATER-SOLUBLE PENCILS

These pencils are a good place to start when you want to be a bit more experimental. They can be applied to the paper in exactly the same way as an ordinary pencil, but then the shading and lines can be blended on the paper with a wet brush. The effect is one of beautifully subtle gradation of tone which cannot be achieved with a dry pencil alone. Working with water-soluble pencils and brushes will give you the confidence to branch out into working with watercolour and other paints.

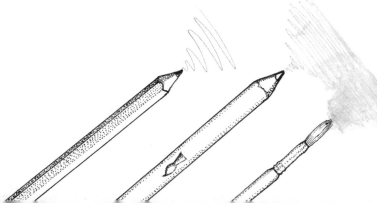

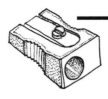

SHARPENERS

Standard lead pencils encased in wood must be kept sharp in order to create a clear line. Always keep a good pencil sharpener to hand and use it as soon as the clarity of your lines decreases. However, blunt, more rounded leads are good for creating soft shading.

PROPELLING PENCILS

These pencils negate the need for a sharpener. They contain fine lengths of lead within a plastic pen-like case. The lead is held in position by a fine metal 'nib' and as it is worn down during the drawing process it can be 'propelled' using a push button at the end of the pencil. Propelling pencils can be filled with any grade of pencil from soft to hard and are great for making precise, clear lines, hatching and cross-hatching.

BLENDING STICKS

Also known as tortillons or paper stumps, these are used for blending shaded areas into a soft gradation of tone. Blending sticks are available from art shops, though you can easily make your own by rolling up a square old newspaper into a pencil shape.

ERASERS

One of the first things you learn about pencil lines when you are a child is that they can be erased, so mistakes are easy to rectify. It is a good idea to have a hard eraser to hand while you draw so that you can immediately correct errors. Putty rubbers are the consistency of plasticine and you can knead them into a fine point with your fingers then apply the point to the paper in a dabbing motion to remove small areas of pencil or charcoal. The precision of the putty rubber makes it a very useful tool to have in your pencil box.

PENS

Beautiful drawings can be created in pen and ink. Pens are available in a huge variety, from fine-nibbed pens to create thin, clear lines and fine hatching and stippling to thick felt-tipped brush pens with which to ink in large areas to establish a saturated intensity of shade. Water-soluble inks can be blended to create subtle gradations.

WORK STATION

A drawing can be created anywhere, whether you're out and about or in the comfort of your home. All you need is a surface which will withstand the pressure of your pencil – be it a sturdy sketch pad or a table – and most importantly a good source of light to illuminate your drawing and your subject. The ideal is to work in daylight and there's nothing more satisfying than sitting outside on a bright day sketching your cat snoozing in the sunshine, but a good source of electric light is the next best thing. Angled desk lamps are great for lighting your work when you're working in the evening.

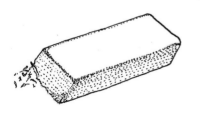

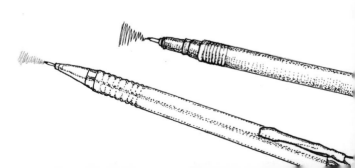

Basic techniques

We were all taught to draw simple shapes in early childhood, but there are many more exciting approaches to making a mark. Drawing is not just about the outline, but what you can do to give your drawings substance and visual realism. Here we shall explore a few of the simple techniques which will prepare you for more advanced exercises later in the book.

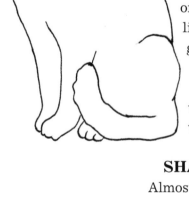

OUTLINES

The outline is generally the starting point for every drawing you will make. It can be sketchy to begin with as you plan the contours of your image then made more definite as you continue to develop ideas of how you want the final picture to look. A well-thought-out outline will ultimately enable you to create a beautiful drawing. When you start to sketch, apply only very light pressure so that the lines are easy to erase if need be. Use greater pressure when you come to drawing in your final outline. At this stage you can begin to think about using shading to add life and solidity to your image.

SHADING AND BLENDING

Almost everyone will be familiar with the back-and-forth strokes of the traditional shading technique. Varying the pressure of the pencil will allow you to control the depth of the shadows. As we explored on p.8, pencil leads are available in a variety of grades. The softer leads will allow you to create darker shadows and blend the edges to gradate the tone.

SHADING GUIDE

It can be useful to create a shading guide that you can refer to when you begin to add tonal value to your drawings. This will help you to see the varying depths of shade and how these might help you to bring your initial outline forms to life.

HATCHING

This simple but effective technique is one of drawing a series of lines parallel to each other. Varying the distance between the lines will alter the tonal effect; closely spaced hatching produces darker tonal values, while increasing the distance between the lines can be used to establish mid-tones. Hatching lines can also be curved; this is a great way of evoking a rounded surface on three-dimensional shapes.

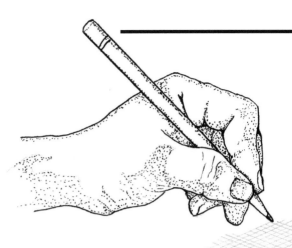

CROSS-HATCHING

Like hatching, this technique is a great way of describing light and shade in your drawings. Start with hatched lines following one direction, then add a series of lines on top of this in a counter-direction. You will achieve a lattice of lines, and as with hatching, varying the distance between the lines will lighten or darken the tonal effect. Cross-hatching also allows you to evoke the three-dimensional shape of the form you are drawing.

STIPPLING

Stippling is a great way of adding controlled tone and texture to your drawings. Simply make a series of dots over the area that needs shading. Play around with your dots, experimenting by varying their size and the distance between them.

SCUMBLING

This technique involves using your pen or pencil to make multiple random looping scribbles over the areas which require tonal shade. The process not only creates tonal contrast but also establishes a texture and adds visual interest to your shadows. You can also achieve a scumbled effect with chalk, charcoal and pastel by lightly rubbing the medium over the paper so that the tone of the paper is still allowed to shine through. This produces the same interesting surface texture as scumbling with a pen or pencil.

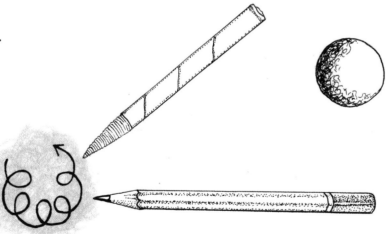

CHAPTER 1

ANATOMY, FORM AND MOVEMENT

Starting to draw anything new may feel like a daunting challenge, but tackled in the right way, learning to draw cats successfully can be very much easier than you might have imagined.

The skeletal structure of any animal is the framework that gives the body its distinctive appearance. Therefore, learning how to draw the shapes of the bones and studying how they fit together is a great way to begin your journey. We shall look at how the form of the cat can be simplified so that starting a sketch is easy, and how to make sure your drawings are proportionally correct. Of course the shape of individual cats varies widely, but once you have learnt some rules about how to plan a drawing of a generic feline form you will be able to adapt your drawings according to the subject before you. As your confidence grows through practice, you will be able to create beautiful images of a standard that you may never have thought possible.

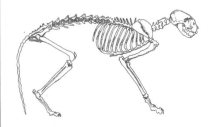

Basic anatomy: understanding the feline form

Understanding what lies beneath the fur and muscles of a cat is the first step towards creating a truly convincing outline and developing dynamic and interesting poses. Knowledge of this structure will allow you to place your shading strategically so that your drawing really comes to life and establishes the illusion of the three-dimensional form upon the paper.

The skeleton anchors the muscles and dictates how the cat can move, so it is important for you to have an idea of how the bones connect at the joints and where the main muscle structures lie to give the cat the distinctive shape we all know. Below are two diagrams displaying the feline skeleton and showing where the muscles are located in relation to these bones. You do not need to have a scientific knowledge of every bone and muscle; just bear in mind the overall shapes and positions when you start a drawing.

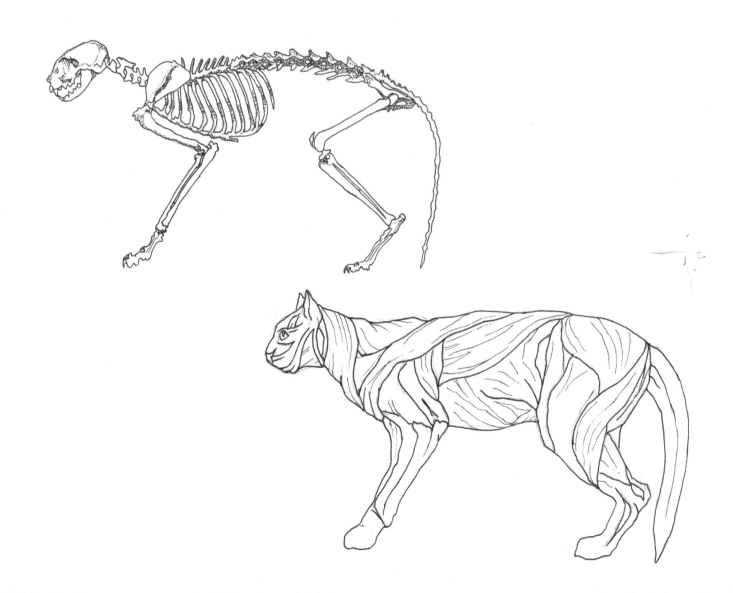

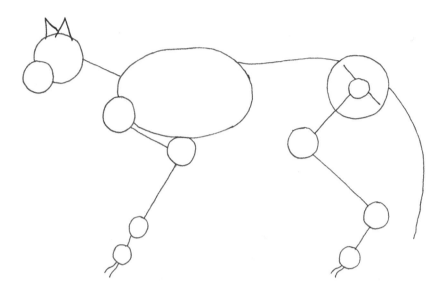

In the final diagram I have highlighted the key joint locations with circles and simplified the bones connecting these joints to mere lines. It is a good idea to copy this diagram, since the process of creating a simple image of the cat's basic form will cement the structure in your mind. You will then always be able to recall it so that you can draw a cat in any position just by adapting the image.

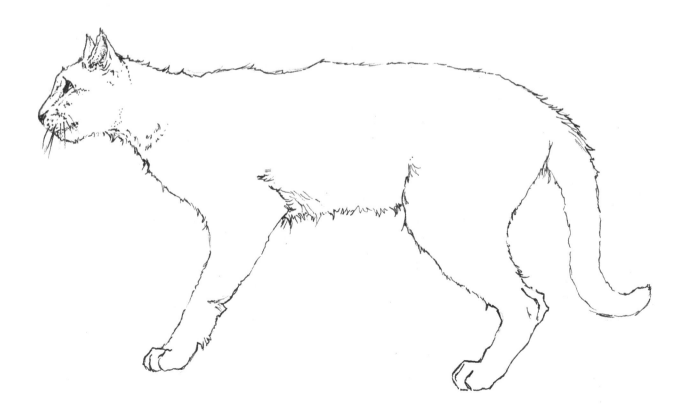

The proportions of the average feline form

We have examined the skeletal structure of the cat and seen how the bones and muscles are positioned beneath the skin. But how do we establish the size of the limbs, body and tail so that our final drawing acquires a harmony and appears 'correct' both in size and shape?

Proportion guideline

There is a simple but effective rule for achieving a correctly proportioned drawing: use the length of the cat's head as a yardstick to work out roughly how big the other body parts should be. This guideline will help you to develop your confidence at the early stages and will eventually enable you to evolve an innate feel for the proportional relationships between the parts of the cat's body so that you will soon be able to do away with this formulaic approach and begin to draw with the instinctive freedom that comes with practice.

Be aware that the proportion of a cat will vary according to each individual and on the position and angle from which it is viewed. This proportional rule is great as a foundation for creating a generic form but it is always important when drawing to look carefully at your subject and adjust your proportions accordingly so that you can really capture the essence and personality of the individual cat.

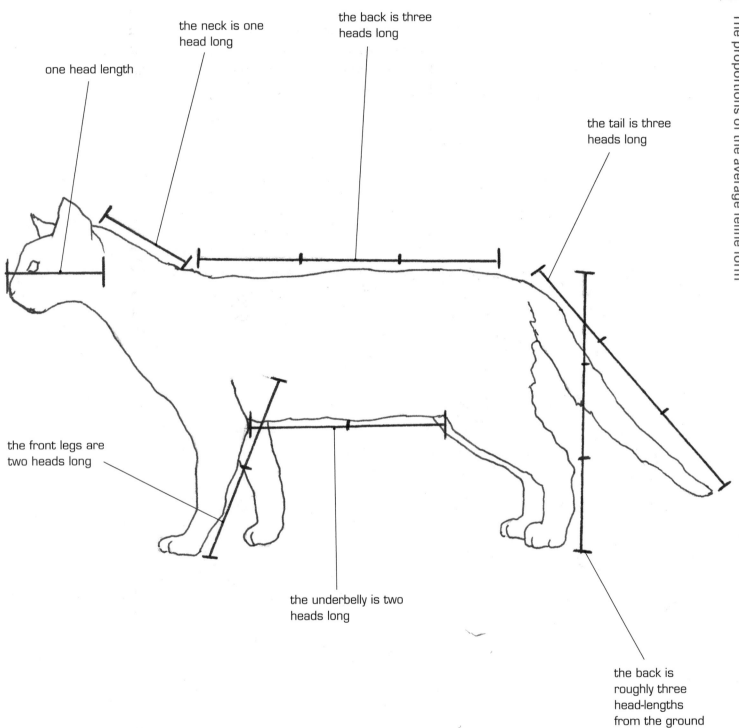

one head length

the neck is one head long

the back is three heads long

the tail is three heads long

the front legs are two heads long

the underbelly is two heads long

the back is roughly three head-lengths from the ground

Using simple shapes to create your outline

The cat has a complex form and each animal also has its own physical characteristics. By breaking down the form into simple shapes with which we are all familiar, you can overcome any anxiety about making a mistake in the crucial early stages of your drawings.

In these drawings I have used rectangles, ovals and circles to build the familiar shape of the cat in various poses. You will see how subtly adjusting the sizes and angular relationships between the shapes enables you to depict the cat in almost any position.

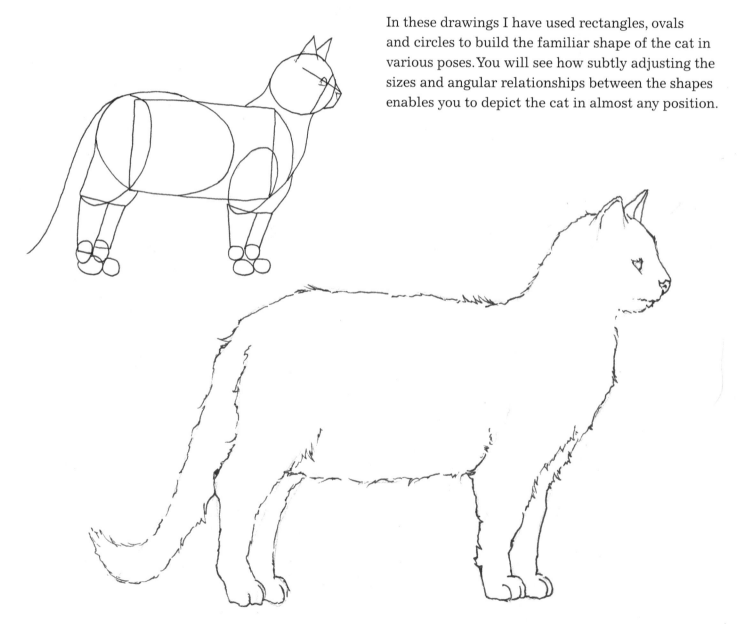

Using simple shapes to create your outline

The skull and face

As we explored earlier in this chapter, the skeleton is the structure that dictates the shapes and final outline of the cat and it is therefore very important to the success of a drawing. Here I have made two sketches of the cat's skull, one from the front and the other in profile. You can see how the skull fits within the outline of the face and how they give it shape.

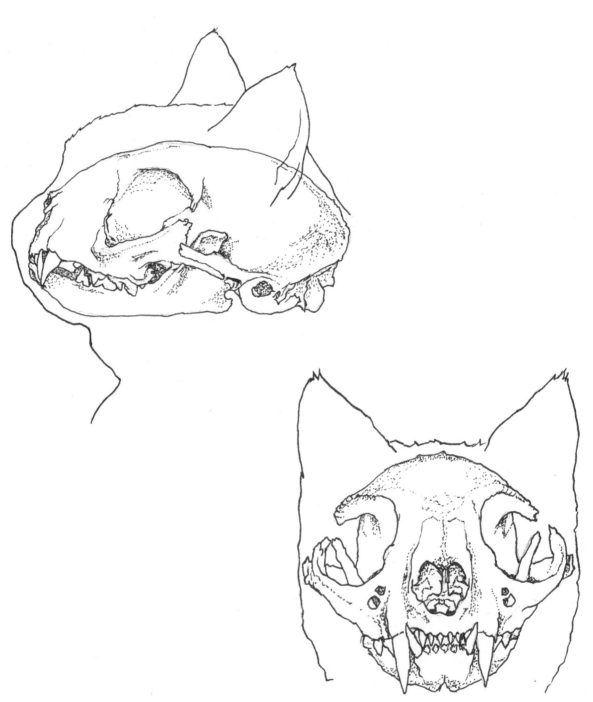

Facial proportions

We have seen in the previous pages how to roughly locate the eyes, nose and mouth upon the cat's face. The step-by-step diagrams shown here explain how you can begin to draw a more sophisticated feline portrait with ease, safe in the knowledge that the positioning of the elements of the face, the overall proportions and the structure of your outline will be correct.

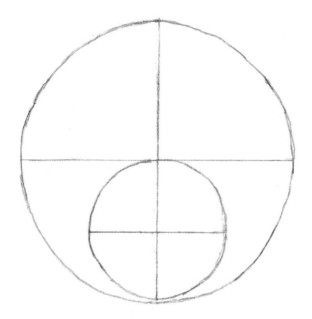

STEP 1

Start by drawing a circle, then divide this circle in half vertically and horizontally. Draw another small circle within the first, between the horizontal dividing line and the bottom of the large circle, then divide this small circle in half vertically and horizontally.

STEP 2

Sketch in the muzzle within the small circle. Use the point at which the horizontal and vertical lines bisect to position an inverted triangle which will become the nose. Extend two curving lines from the bottom of the triangle – these will become the top of the cat's mouth. Extend two lines upwards from the top corners of the triangle to establish the bridge of the nose. Finally, draw in the outer edges of the muzzle using the small circle as a guide.

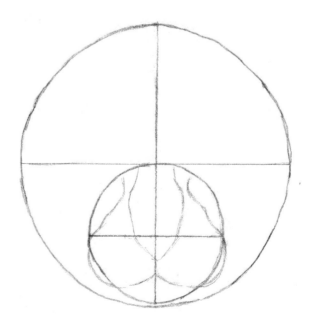

STEP 3

By adding a few more vertical and horizontal guidelines you can confidently sketch in the eyes, above and on each side of the muzzle. Now extend lines from the main horizontal line, starting from the line you used to establish the top of the eyes. These lines will help you map out the position of the ear tips; make sure the lines are the same length. Now draw in two triangles (which will become the ears) by using the ends of your angled lines as the apex of the triangle. Finally, sketch in two more angled lines at the bottom of the large circle to establish the jawline contour.

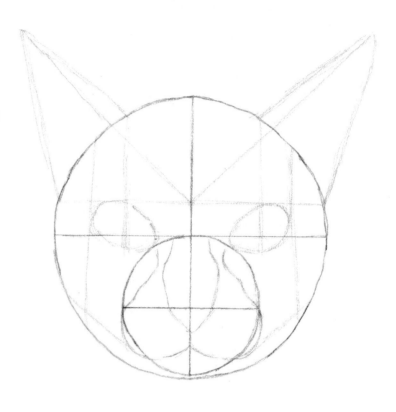

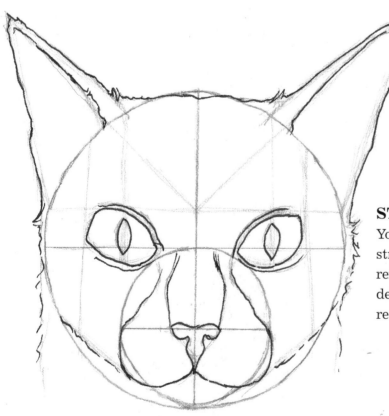

STEP 4

You now have your basic facial structure and can move on to refining the outline and adding detail to the features to create a realistic portrait.

Drawing the face at different angles

Now that you are familiar with the basic rules for correctly placing the facial features of the cat, it will be easy to tackle drawing the cat's portrait at different angles. I have drawn three simple diagrams depicting the face from the front, side and three-quarter profile. With these basic structures established it is easy to refine the outline and add tonal and textural variation to produce a simple but effective portrait sketch.

CHAPTER 2

EXPLORING DETAIL

You should now be confident in your ability to draw a cat with its form proportionally correct, so it is time to look at the separate elements of the feline body more closely. Adding detail to your basic outlines will bring character and individuality to your drawings, allowing you to create recognizable portraits of beloved pets.

In this chapter we shall look at how to adapt the shapes of facial features to create familiar expressions such as alertness, sleepiness, anger and relaxation. You will discover how to build your drawings so that they are not just two-dimensional sketches but portraits with real soul and emotion – images that convey the essence and character of individual cats.

The eyes

Cats are natural hunters and as such they have excellent eyesight. Their hunting activities often take place at night-time and for this reason their eyes have big lenses and extremely sensitive retinas which gives them far superior nocturnal vision to that of humans. They are also active in the daytime, of course, and need a way of protecting their retinas from strong sunlight; the solution is the distinctive vertical slit-like pupils. The pupils open very wide at night-time to maximize the amount of light entering the eye, thus improving vision; they close to a narrow opening to restrict strong light entering through the pupil and prevent the retina from being damaged.

This labelled diagram shows all the key elements you will need to be aware of when drawing cats' eyes.

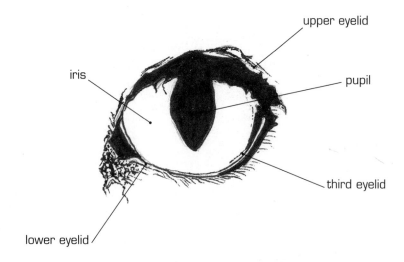

upper eyelid

iris

pupil

third eyelid

lower eyelid

Drawing the eye: step by step

As you have discovered from the previous chapter, when you are starting to tackle a new subject matter in your drawing it is always easier to break down your subject into simple shapes as it makes tackling a complicated form far less daunting. The following step-by-step sequence of drawings will guide you through drawing the cat's eyes from the front.

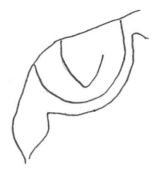

STEP 1

I started by drawing two almond shapes about 3 cm (1¼ in) apart. I shaped the inner corners of the almonds down into an inverted tapering teardrop. Within this initial shape I then drew in a circle that will become the iris. Finally, within this, I sketched the pupil using another almond shape, positioned vertically.

STEP 2

I continued by adding variation and texture to my initial outline. I then sketched the areas within the pupil that will become the reflective highlights. These highlights are really important when drawing an eye because they add depth and tonal contrast to your image, creating the impression of a shiny, liquid surface, a quality that every eye possesses.

STEP 3

Use this stage of the drawing to establish the darkest tones of the eye. For a striking tonal contrast and an intense visual impact, I used a black felt pen, but you can also use a soft-leaded pencil (6B or 8B) as this will also produce a deep intensity of tone.

When colouring in the pupils I made sure to leave the highlights untouched, allowing the white paper to shine out in contrast to the dark tone. I used a little stippling to gradate the edges of the highlights.

STEP 4

With the most important tonal areas established in the previous step, I then added more textural and tonal detail around the eyes.

Using the eyes to express emotion

The eyes are generally the first place we look when we want to establish communication as they are hugely important in gauging what someone is feeling. This is the reason why they are often referred to as the windows to the soul. What is true of people is also true of cats! Learning how to draw the eyes so that they can convey a recognizable emotion or state of mind will allow you to create drawings with real meaning and substance. Simply adapt the shapes we used in the previous step-by-step example to imbue your cat drawings with individuality and really bring an expression to life.

Sleepy eyes

In this drawing the eyes are totally closed; all that can be seen are dark slits where the upper and lower eyelid meet. The hatched line detail unifies the eyes and adds to the calm, sleepy appearance of the drawing.

Alert eyes

These eyes are so wide they are almost circular. Edging the iris with a dark border further emphasizes the feeling of intent concentration and watchfulness. The pupils are thin slits and the highlights are tiny pin-pricks, both of these elements enhancing the wideness of the eyes. A little attention to textural detail around the eyes sets them in the context of the face.

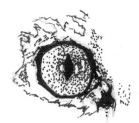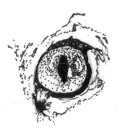

Angry eyes

By narrowing the eyes slightly at the inner corners and widening the outer corners you can create an aggressive, intense, squinting expression. A thick dark border on the upper eyelid and stark white highlights in the middle of the wide dark pupils makes the expression unmistakable – this is definitely a cat not to be messed with!

The ears

A cat's hearing is probably even more finely tuned than its eyesight. Cats are commonly thought to possess a 'sixth sense', but it is more probable that their hearing is so good they can detect a presence or occurrence from a tiny movement, one that would simply go undetected by us humans. A cat's ears are therefore extremely important. The good news is that depicting them is relatively easy – if you can draw a triangle, you will be able to draw a cat's ear.

The ear as simple shapes

The examples here show you how to draw a simple outline of the ear, seen from the front, the side and the back. You will see that all the drawings start with a circular foundation shape. Straight lines are added to help establish the outline of the ear. Copying these simple examples will help you to draw a realistic ear from any angle. You will soon acquire a natural feel for the shape and dimensions of the ear so that you can sketch freely by closely observing your subject.

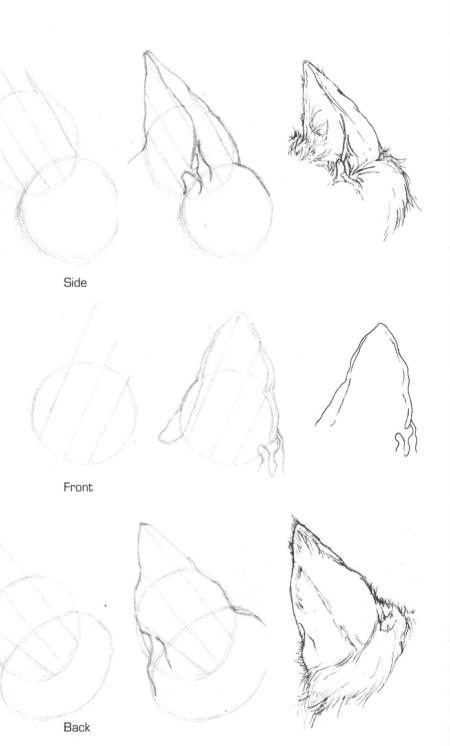

Side

Front

Back

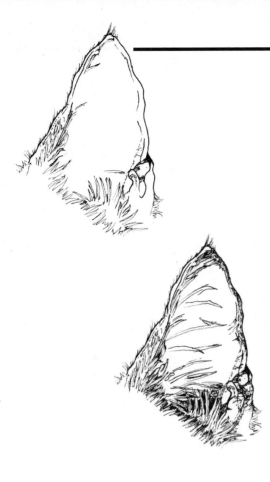

Building texture and tone into your outline

These additional three steps build upon the outline of the ear seen from the front. You can see how easy it is to add substance and texture to your simple outlines.

Conveying mood with the ears

Like the eyes, the ears are a great way of conveying the mood of your subject. Here I have drawn three detailed examples of a cat's ears in different positions. In the first drawing, the ears are flattened, demonstrating anger or irritation. The central drawing shows the cat's ears from behind; they are upright but not pricked, showing that the cat is relaxed. In the final drawing they are pricked up, alert – something has piqued this cat's interest!

The nose

A cat's sense of smell is fourteen times stronger than that of a human. It is important for finding food, locating a mate and, most vitally, sniffing out danger. So while the cat's nose might be small, it performs a major function.

The following step-by-step examples demonstrate how to draw a nose from the front and the side using a few simple but effective stages.

The nose seen from the front

STEP 1

Start by drawing a diamond shape (above). Sketch in a short line extending from the lower point of the diamond, dividing the bottom of the shape in half vertically.

STEP 2

Extend two curved lines from the upper point of the diamond, bringing them back round to meet the upper sides of the diamond shape about halfway down. You have now created the basic shape of the cat's nostrils.

STEP 3

Add some broken sketchy lines beneath the nostrils, suggesting the fur texture. Now extend two curved lines from the lower tip of the diamond; these lines will become the upper lip.

STEP 4

Strengthen your outline and erase your construction lines. Establish the darkest tones in the nostril cavities. Use a little stippling to gradate the tonal range from dark to light.

STEP 5

Finally, add some more sketchy lines to develop the furry texture around the nose. Add a little sparse stippling to give the skin of the nose a three-dimensional quality.

The nose seen from the side

STEP 1

Draw a triangle shape with the upper point squared off. This shape will act as a framework upon which you can build the nose.

STEP 2

Refine the outline of the basic triangle and extend a line at an oblique angle from the upper vertical. This will become the top of the cat's nose.

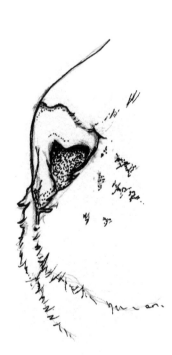

STEP 3

Sketch in lines beneath the nose to suggest the furry muzzle of the cat. Darken the nostril cavity, strengthen your initial outline and add some shading to suggest the roots of the whiskers.

STEP 4

Add some sketchy lines to develop the furry texture of the muzzle and finally draw in some whiskers. These really bring life to the drawing and add character to the muzzle.

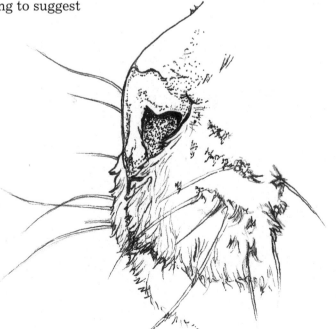

Combining facial detail: a cat portrait

Now you have learnt how to draw the separate elements of a cat's head, it is time to combine them and create a cat portrait by mapping out the basic form of the head and then developing the detail of the eyes, ears, nose and mouth.

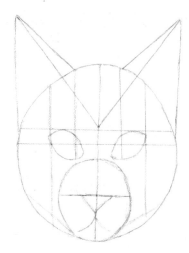

STEP 1

Lay out the structure and proportion of your cat's face using the step-by-step approach we looked at on pp.21–2. This will give you the basic framework upon which to develop detail and imbue your drawing with the essential character of your subject.

STEP 2

Using this linear structure as a rough guide, sketch in the outline of your cat's face. Use this stage to add some of the fur texture and refine the outlines of the eyes, nose and mouth.

STEP 3

Strengthen these refined outlines and erase your structural working lines.

STEP 4

Shade the pupils and lids of the eyes and start to sketch in the fur markings. Stipple some dots upon the muzzle; when you come to draw in the whiskers, these dots will allow you to draw the root of each whisker in the right place.

STEP 5

Shade in the markings upon the forehead and around the eyes and add sketchy lines and stippling to the insides of the ears; these lines evoke the long hairs that protect the inner ear from dust and dirt. The stippling creates a mid-tonal shadow which begins to suggest the concavity of the ears.

STEP 6

Add some more sketchy texture lines to unify the dark markings with the lighter areas, bringing the separate elements of the face together. Finally, add the gently curving lines of the whiskers on the muzzle and above the eyes to complete your portrait.

Capturing emotion: facial expressions

Just as with humans, a cat's state of mind can be determined by reading its facial expression and it is amazing how easily we can gauge the mood of our feline friends. Learning the key features which indicate a particular expression will help you when you are trying to convey emotion in your drawings. On these pages you can see how the shape of the eyes, nose, mouth and ears changes according to the cat's mood.

When making studies in pencil I like to keep things simple: there is no need to have a huge variety of pencils at your disposal. A soft lead to create dark, dense shadow and a harder lead to establish thin clear lines and light and shade is all that is required. I like Derwent sketching pencils, using an HB pencil for the lighter shadows and an 8B for the darker tones.

Sleepy

Sleepy cats are fantastic subjects to draw when you are starting out. As any cat owner will know, once your pet is snuggled down in a comfortable spot it is unlikely to move for the next few hours. This gives you plenty of time to record its facial features in your sketches. I did this sketch while my cat was sunbathing on the sofa – you really know a cat is out for the count when you can see its little tongue poking out!

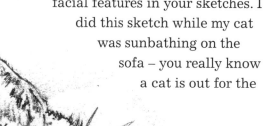

I wanted to keep this study tonally soft to accentuate the feeling of relaxation. I used an HB pencil throughout, making sure the lead was sharpened to a point so that I was able to achieve a clear outline. Once I was happy with the form of my cat I worked on indicating the pattern of the fur, constantly referring to my sleeping subject during this process and using small circular scumbling movements to apply the pencil to the paper. This process really helps to suggest the three-dimensional presence of the cat.

Yawning

A yawning cat is sweetly comical. I made
this sketch from a photograph I had taken
of a cat just as it was waking up from a
long nap. I sketched in the outline with an
HB pencil and applied my 8B pencil firmly
to the paper to produce the dark tones
around the eyes and the pattern of the fur.
I then used my HB pencil to lightly scumble
in a half-tone to show the texture of the
rest of the cat's face.

Alert

Our tame domestic cats still possess the hunting instincts of their wild relatives. This sketch shows the wide eyes and pricked ears of a cat whose attention has been caught by something interesting. I have accentuated this idea of attentiveness by leaving large white highlights in the eyes to focus the viewer upon the cat's alert engagement.

I wanted this study to have clarity and contrast to convey the idea of sharp watchfulness. I therefore used the same HB pencil to sketch in the outline of the cat but when elaborating upon the details I used a softer 8B pencil, which makes the eyes and fur pattern of the cat stand out as a strong dark tone against the white of the paper. I used a firm pressure to apply the pencil to the paper and this really intensifies the depth of the tone.

Angry

No one messes with a grumpy cat unless they are brave or foolhardy. Their angry expression is unmistakable: ears back, eyes narrowed, mouth open and teeth bared – a cat that means business!

I felt the focus of this study needed to be the eyes and the open mouth, because these are the features that really evoke the anger of the cat. So, once I had sketched in the basic outline with an HB pencil, I began to darken the pupils of the eyes and the interior of the mouth. I made sure I left the exposed teeth white so that they stood out against the dark background. To finish the drawing I added the fur pattern across the top of the head using the HB pencil.

Playful

All young animals learn through play, and it is wonderful to watch a litter of kittens play-fighting with each other. I was lucky enough to spend the afternoon with a friend's kitten and at only four months old she was full of fun and mischief! She had a great time playing with a length of string which we dangled above her head and teased her with. I did this drawing from a photograph I took – I love her concentrated expression as she bats at the string with her little paw.

I wanted to create a tonal balance in this sketch, with clarity of line but not as much contrast as in the alert cat. I began sketching the outline with an HB pencil, then, using the same pencil, I worked at creating the surface texture of the fluffy face. Next, taking the 8B pencil, I picked out the darker markings upon the fur and darkened the tone of the eyes. I left the uplifted paw quite light so that it is thrown into focus against the patterned fur behind it.

Body details

We have examined in detail all the key facial features of the cat so that you can build a head portrait. Now it's time to take a look at a few of the other elements of the cat, that can, at first, seem a little tricky to draw.

The paws

These step-by-step drawings show how simple it is to draw a paw and lower leg. Take the approach we examined in the first chapter, using circles to locate the positions of the joints and straight lines to form the basis of the connecting bones.

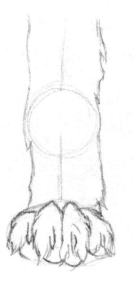

These drawings show the difference between the front and hind paws (left to right), seen from below.

The tail

A cat's tail is used for more than just balance. It is yet another way your cat can communicate, both with you and other animals. I have drawn three tails here to demonstrate the different emotions a cat can display.

The tail held high in the air with a slightly curving tip signifies that your cat is friendly and wants some attention, but is at the same time still a little tentative.

When the tail is held low down behind the cat's rear legs, watch out! The cat is not happy and is in a defensive or potentially aggressive mood.

The tail curled up over the back shows the cat is happy and probably enjoying a stroke. All cats love undivided attention – when it suits them, of course!

Combining body details

You are now ready to use all that you have learnt about drawing the separate features to create a drawing of a cat in its entirety. Making a detailed drawing is not difficult – it may seem like a daunting task at first, but we have tackled each separate feature of the cat and explored how simple shapes can be combined. Using this gradual approach and tackling each element in simple stages has allowed you to familiarize yourself with everything you need to make a successful drawing of a whole cat.

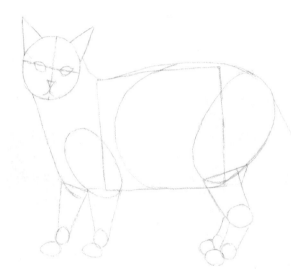

STEP 1

Construct the form of your cat using the simple shapes we looked at in Chapter 1. Also check the proportions of the limbs, tail and back of the cat.

STEP 2

Use this basic diagram to develop a more natural outline for your cat.

STEP 3

Erase your preliminary
construction lines and
begin to add detail to the
eyes, nose and ears. Start
to develop some texture
around the facial features
to draw the face together.

STEP 4

Continue adding sketchy hatched lines to
develop the fur texture. Add hatched lines
to the farther front and hind legs so that it
becomes clear that these legs are set back
from those in the foreground. This shading
really starts to evolve your drawing into a
substantial three-dimensional form.

STEP 5

Add more strategically
placed sketchy hatched
lines to the edges of the
cat's body, tail and legs.
This subtle working
unifies the whole drawing,
bringing together all the
separate features which
you have been working on.

CHAPTER 3

DRAWING FROM LIFE AND FROM PHOTOGRAPHS

When you first start drawing, one of the big questions that may trouble you is whether you should work from a photograph or from first-hand observation of life. But there is no 'should' when it comes to creating art; every drawing is an expression. What is so liberating about the process of drawing is that there is no right or wrong; your technique and ability will improve with practice no matter how you work. Using a photograph as a reference is just as valid as working from a real-life model – the two approaches are very different but both can enable you to create beautiful cat drawings. In this chapter we shall examine how to begin sketching from life and how photographs can be used in many different ways to help you create original drawings.

Sketching from life

When sketching from life you need to be quick. Don't be precious about your marks or worry about a line being in the wrong place – just draw! The most important thing is that you get your form started on the paper; look at the results as scribbled notes, or a pictorial *aide-memoire*. Move around your subject and record how it looks from many different angles, working fast and covering your page with sketches. This might sound a little haphazard, but these sketching exercises are really liberating – they free you up, render you unafraid to make errors and allow you to sift through reams of sketches so that you can see elements of your drawings that are really successful and can be reused in later works.

If you have followed the more formal approaches to creating cats in the previous chapters you will find that they have been absorbed into the way you draw from now on. The only equipment I needed for this drawing session was an HB pencil and an eraser, so this exercise really couldn't be simpler!

As any cat owner knows, unless a cat is sleeping it cannot be guaranteed to stay in the same position for long. Consequently, a snoozing cat is a great subject when you start your experiments with drawing from life.

I spent the afternoon with two very sleepy cats, sketching them separately and together; they were from the same litter of kittens so they love to snuggle up to each other. They were somewhat fidgety, even though they were sleeping, which was useful because it meant I could record their forms in several different positions.

I filled nearly half a sketchbook with very quick sketches, some taking me only 30 seconds. I have selected a few examples here. Note how my use of line is free and light; although there are no hard edges around the forms, you can still see the simple shapes which I used to plan the outlines of my cats. These are by no means finished drawings – they are visual notes which I will be able to develop so that I can create a beautiful portrait of these two handsome cats.

From sketch to finished drawing

I sifted through my sketches and decided upon the composition I thought most effective. I wanted to do a finished drawing with both the cats asleep together. Not only does this give the drawing the obvious appeal of having two gorgeous cats to look at instead of one, I also felt it was more interesting and challenging to show their close, affectionate relationship and the separate personalities of each individual.

Here is the sketch which inspired me and from which my final drawing evolved. I loved this pose in particular because the legs and tails form a unifying zig-zag pattern which interlocks the two cats. I also liked the proximity of their faces – they look peaceful and relaxed, intertwined in a trusting embrace.

STEP 1

Using my quick sketch as a formal reference, I began to draw a more detailed outline. While I drew I constantly referred to the cats from life as well as using my sketch. This enabled me to elaborate on details – the structure of the ears, the shape of the paws and the position of the fur markings.

STEP 2

I wanted to set the sleeping cats in context with
their surroundings so, using their bed as reference,
I began to sketch in some rough lines to show the
folds of cloth around the bodies of the cats. This
done, the drawing was really beginning to come
to life. Now I wanted to add some tone to the
linear sketch. The cat on the left, Barney, is a very
dark tortoiseshell and Bumble is white and pale
ginger, so they are tonally very different and this
gives a fantastic visual contrast. At this stage of
my drawing the cats had moved apart and were
sleeping in separate areas of the room, so I sat in
front of each cat in turn and shaded in the facial
detail, referring constantly to my subject.

Drawing from life and from photographs

STEP 3

Having established the tonal and textural detail of the faces I could then gauge the tonal levels of each cat and how the difference in tone would demarcate them as two separate forms. From this point on I wanted to work on each cat separately, mainly so that I didn't have to go backwards and forwards between the separate rooms they were now occupying, but also because I wanted to achieve a visual cohesion to make it clear which body parts belonged to which cat. I started with the darker cat as that would allow me to determine the lighter tone of the ginger and white cat to make a good contrast. I worked quickly, almost scribbling the pencil over the paper, which allowed me to achieve a dark tone as well as the texture of the fur. I was careful to leave light areas to vary the surface of the body and of course replicate the actual markings of the cat.

STEP 4

After I finished working on Barney's drawing, I went off in search of Bumble. Luckily he was still very sleepy, sunbathing in front of a window. I positioned myself strategically so that all the details of his body that I needed to see in order to complete his portrait were visible. I wanted to establish his light mid-tone early, so very quickly and lightly I shaded in all the coloured areas of his fur, leaving his white back leg untouched. Using my finger, I gently smudged this shading to a smooth finish. I then began to add the darker stripes of the fur pattern over this shading. Finally I added some light texture shading to the white back leg. Now the drawing was really beginning to come together.

STEP 5

All that was left to do was to set the sleeping pair within their environment. I very quickly added some lightly shaded areas around the cats and smoothed this shading with my finger. I darkened some areas within the shading to suggests deeper folds in the fabric of their bedding.

Using photographs as reference

Taking photographs is the easiest way of recording a subject that has attracted you and these can be used to inspire a new drawing. While sketching from life does have the benefit of allowing you to gain a three-dimensional view of your subject, using a photograph as a reference when drawing a mobile subject such as a cat can make a difficult task much easier. Photographs also allow you to start experimenting with drawing more dynamic poses – a running cat, or a brief moment of interaction between a group of cats.

Squaring up your photograph

The easiest way to translate the shapes and proportions in a photograph accurately into your drawing is to use a grid system of lines drawn over your reference image. The boxes of your grid should all be the same size, so use a ruler to accurately measure out your grid.

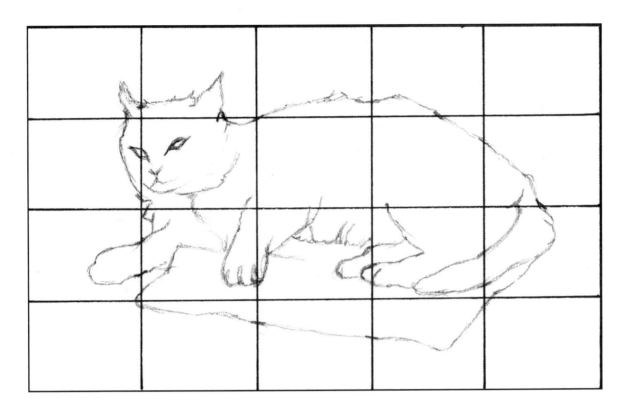

Once you have a photograph with a clear grid, prepare the paper upon which you want to make your drawing. You must now draw another grid with the same number of squares vertically and horizontally. These can be the same size as the grid on the photograph or proportionally bigger or smaller. So, for example, if the grid squares on your photograph measure 2 × 2 cm (¾ × ¾ in) and you want your drawing to be twice the size of the original image, make your squares 4 × 4 cm (1½ × 1½ in). Draw the grid on your paper very lightly in pencil so that the lines can be erased once you are happy with the outlines of your drawing.

Once you have the grid drawn up on your paper you can start drawing. Look carefully at your photograph and note where outlines of the form intersect with the grid, then make markers in corresponding intersections on the grid of your paper. Once you have a series of markers all over the grid, you can then begin to link up these points and create a fairly accurate outline.

Mother and kittens: drawing movement

For this project I wanted to exploit the way photographs preserve a transient image, so I chose a subject that would be very difficult to draw from life. Kittens are extremely fidgety subjects, even more so than adult cats, and this is where photographic reference material becomes a great boon. In this photograph a mother cat reclines with one kitten standing close by, while the other strides purposefully towards her.

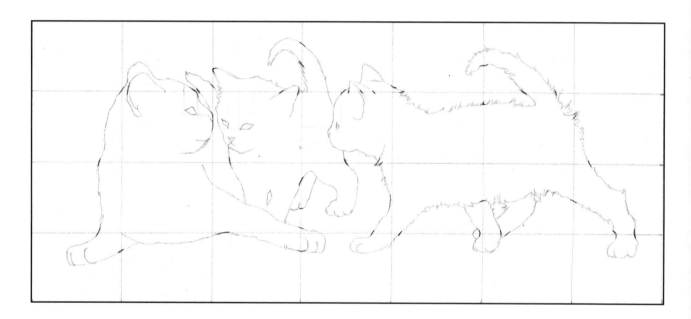

STEP 1

Using the squaring-up method, I marked the points on the grid where the forms of the cats cross the lines. With these markers as a guide, I then lightly sketched in the preliminary outline of my drawing.

STEP 2

Using a fine-nibbed pen, I went over my
pencil outline, refining the detail and
making slight alterations. I was then able
to erase all the pencil working and was left
with a beautifully clear outline.

STEP 3

I began adding texture and tone to the
bodies of the cats with a pencil, constantly
referring to my photograph to accurately
place the markings on the cats' fur. I used
the fairly hard 2B pencil so that at this
early stage I could keep the tonal feel of the
picture quite light.

STEP 4

I continued working up the detail of the fur over all three cats and then began to vary the tone, darkening shadows in between crevices. This helped to solidify the group and give them a real presence and unity. For the darkest shadows I used an 8B pencil. The softer lead allowed really dark intensity to be established in the drawing.

STEP 5

Finally, I softly shaded some light shadows beneath the bodies and paws of the cats. This addition of cast shadow anchors the group to the ground, placing them within a physical context.

Finding inspiration: visiting a cat rescue centre

You may not have your own fabulous feline waiting for you when you return home, but this need not put you off your adventures into drawing cats from life. There are plenty of rescue centres looking after abandoned and homeless cats and visiting one of these could be just the thing to inspire you.

I phoned my nearest rescue centre and was invited to spend the afternoon exploring their facilities. It was a wonderful experience and I got to see and make friends with a large number of cats. I made dozens of sketches and took many photographs. What I loved about making the sketches was the variety of shapes and sizes – kittens, old cats, fluffy cats, smooth-haired cats, all sorts of colours and patterns. Being surrounded by so many different cats gives so much scope to find a new visual quality which can be used to sum up the essence of a particular cat.

CHAPTER 4

EXPERIMENTING WITH MATERIALS

Now that you have learnt how to depict the form and fur of cats both from life and from photographs, it is time to start experimenting with materials. We are all familiar with the humble pencil and pen, items with which we began to make our first drawings in early childhood, and the previous three chapters have shown what excellent results can be achieved using these simple pieces of equipment. But learning is all about expanding our horizons, trying new things and perfecting new techniques.

So in this chapter we shall go through a series of step-by-step drawings, each created with a new medium. We shall see how a judicious choice of medium can really accentuate the visual character of a particular cat and create a beautiful drawing to a professional standard. With each project we shall also explore a variety of different stylistic approaches, from bold graphic images to more painterly techniques.

Charcoal and chalk techniques

Charcoal is a great medium to start with when you are ready to try out different materials because it is handled in very much the same way as a pencil. It can be used both to create clear lines and to block in areas of shading. You can smudge charcoal and gradate shaded areas with a tortillon or your finger. For highlights, the ideal medium to use in conjunction with it is white chalk.

It is a good idea to use a paper with a grain when working with charcoal and chalk to provide a 'tooth' that the pigment can adhere to. Spraying your finished charcoal drawings with a fixative will prevent smudging and preserve your work.

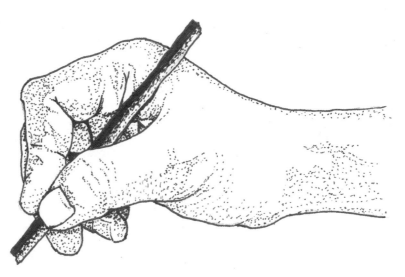

Willow charcoal

Created by charring willow sticks, this is great for creating very quick sketches when drawing from life. Willow charcoal is very soft and excellent for subtle shading as it is very easy to blend with either a finger or tortillon. It can also be erased easily with a putty rubber. You can create highlights in shaded areas by dabbing your paper surface with the putty rubber.

Willow charcoal

Compressed
charcoal

Cross-hatching with
compressed charcoal

Compressed charcoal sticks and charcoal pencils

Compressed charcoal is made of powdered charcoal which is reconstituted into sticks, held together with a gum binder. This charcoal is also available in a pencil form and can be easily sharpened to a point. Charcoal pencils are a great medium to start with. They are much darker and more permanent than willow charcoal, so mistakes are not so easy to erase.

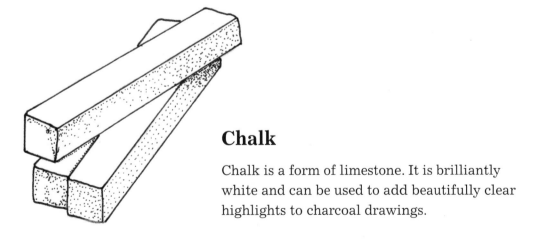

Chalk

Chalk is a form of limestone. It is brilliantly white and can be used to add beautifully clear highlights to charcoal drawings.

Grey kittens: soft, fluffy texture

There is nothing quite like the feel of stroking a young kitten, and with this drawing I wanted to evoke the soft and fluffy texture of the fur. I also aimed to capture that special cheeky look that every kitten has sparkling in its eyes. I decided to make the eyes the centre of my composition, surrounded by the luxurious fur. I was lucky enough to spend some time with two beautiful kittens, so I made numerous quick sketches of them and also took some snaps. I photographed each kitten separately and managed to coax them into sitting up, looking straight forward to make eye contact with me – food treats are always useful to get animals to do what you want!

Materials

- 160 gsm (98 lb) fine grain pastel paper
- willow charcoal
- compressed charcoal pencil
- white chalk
- putty rubber
- tortillon
- fixative

STEP 1

Using my photographs of the kittens as reference images, I began to plan my composition. I wanted the kittens to be close to each other but not touching, so I made sure there was a clear margin between their bodies. I sketched in their outlines using a stick of willow charcoal. This charcoal is very soft, so mistakes are easy to correct with a putty rubber.

STEP 2

I shaded the bodies of the kittens with the willow charcoal, rubbing the stick softly over the surface of the paper. Using my finger, I gently blended the shading to a light grey, smooth, even finish. I then began to darken the shading beneath the kittens' paws.

STEP 3

I sharpened my charcoal pencil to a fine point and added dark lines around the eyes, the pupils and the noses of the kittens. The charcoal pencil mark is darker than the willow charcoal and can therefore produce a more saturated, intense tone. I shaded the irises of the eyes using the point of my tortillon. I was careful to leave a little white dot in the centre of each eye to bring life and sparkle to the kittens' expressions. I then darkened and defined the fur detail around their chests, ears and legs.

STEP 4

Then I began to work on the texture of the kittens' fur. Taking my putty rubber and moulding it into a wedge shape with my fingers, I began to erase highlights into the soft grey shading on their bodies. I drew the rubber's edge over the surface of the paper, using quick, flicking strokes, paying attention to the direction in which the fur was growing. This process began to make the kittens come alive as tangible three-dimensional forms.

STEP 5

Taking the willow charcoal stick, I darkened some of the areas of fur in between my highlights. With my charcoal pencil, I stippled in the dots on the muzzles of the kittens; these little dots would help to position the whiskers. To finish the composition I simply added a few more highlights with my putty rubber to denote the whiskers. I used my chalk to heighten some of the highlights upon the bodies and then, to unite the pair, I added some light shading with the willow charcoal beneath the kittens' paws and blended it to a subtle finish with my finger. Finally, I sprayed the drawing with fixative to prevent it from smudging.

Watercolour and water-soluble pencil techniques

Watercolour paints are inexpensive, light and easy to transport. All you need is a little water and some brushes to bring them to life! They are just as easy to use outdoors on location as they are at home and are therefore a perfect medium for painting nature and animals out in the open. Much of the magic of the technique happens as a result of the little quirks of the medium – happy accidents that occur when the pigment bleeds and blurs on the wet surface of the paper. However, there are a few basic techniques which will allow you to assert some control over your work without suffocating the natural purity and fluidity of the watercolour aesthetic.

Watercolour paints

You can buy watercolour paints either in tubes or in the form of small hard cubes of pigment, known as pans. Either way, all you need is water to dilute the pigment. The more water you use, the lighter and more translucent your paint solution will be.

Paper

Adding water to ordinary paper will make it wrinkle and soften, so it is essential to use paper designed for watercolour painting. This is thicker, denser and has a slight texture to its surface. It is robust enough to withstand saturation and maintain its form. Look out for paper with a weight of 300 gsm (140 lb) or above.

Water-soluble pencils

Just like regular pencils, these are graded according to the density of their leads – an 8B pencil will produce an intense dark tone, while an HB pencil can be used for light washes. Simply apply the pencil to the paper where you want to add some shade and then, using a moist brush, blend the shading. You can achieve really smooth and subtle gradations of tone.

Brushes

It is a good idea to have a variety of different sizes and shapes of brush, including wide, flat brushes for blocking in base washes and round brushes with a pointed tip for creating fine detail.

The wash

This is the most basic technique, forming the basis of probably every watercolour painting you will create. Washes are best applied with a wide flat brush and are used to block in an area of your drawing with tone. There are two types of wash, flat and gradated. The flat wash is tonally even and is applied using horizontal strokes, each brush stroke loaded with the same amount of pigment in order to maintain consistency of tone. The gradated wash, as the name suggests, fades from dark to light, so with each horizontal stroke you need to make sure your brush is loaded with an increasingly dilute pigment solution. Washes are a great way to start your drawings, creating a tone to work into. Make sure you allow base washes to dry thoroughly before working into them to avoid smudging.

Wet-on-dry technique

This technique is very much like drawing with a pen or pencil; it is about creating a clear, crisp line which stands out and contrasts with its background. When executing this technique, make sure you load your brush with a pigment-heavy paint solution; you want your lines to be opaque and clear, not translucent and blurry as with the wet-on-wet technique (see below). A round brush is best for creating sharp lines.

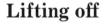

Lifting off

One of the excellent qualities of watercolour paint is that it can be redissolved and lifted from the paper even when it has dried. Simply wet the area of paint you want to remove and with a piece of rag or kitchen paper blot away the moistened pigment. This technique is great for adding texture and visual interest to flat washes.

Wet-on-wet technique

The effect of wet-on-wet technique is beautifully soft and subtle, with undefined areas of tone that bleed into each other. It is achieved by wetting the paper liberally with a wide flat brush and then dropping pigment on to the surface. The more you saturate the surface of your paper the more the pigment will bleed and blur.

Kitten playing: subtle impressionism

Watercolour is a wonderfully spontaneous medium, great for capturing fleeting impressions of a subject by subtle suggestions of tone and form using light, flowing gradations of paint. Half of the beauty of painting with watercolour is letting the watery pigment flow and seeing what fortunate accidents occur.

For this first project working with watercolour I wanted a subject with vitality and energy to reflect the spontaneity of the medium, and what has more energy than a playful kitten? I made this painting from a photograph; I loved the intensity of expression on the kitten's face and the way the front paws are extending ready to capture the toy.

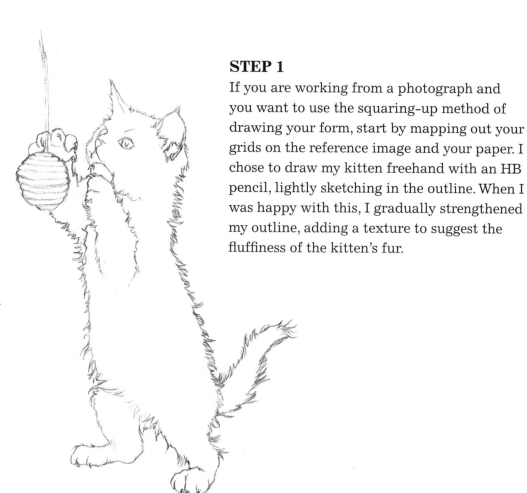

STEP 1

If you are working from a photograph and you want to use the squaring-up method of drawing your form, start by mapping out your grids on the reference image and your paper. I chose to draw my kitten freehand with an HB pencil, lightly sketching in the outline. When I was happy with this, I gradually strengthened my outline, adding a texture to suggest the fluffiness of the kitten's fur.

Materials

- 300 gsm (140 lb) watercolour paper
- HB pencil
- black and Payne's grey watercolour pans
- size 4 round brush

STEP 2

Taking my brush, I mixed a very dilute paint solution using the grey watercolour. Test your own mix on a piece of scrap paper to check the tone before starting. It should be a transparent light grey; with watercolour you should always work from light to dark gradually, since highlights can only be achieved by letting the white of the paper shine through. Once I was happy with the tone of my paint solution, I began to brush on the markings of the kitten's fur and features.

STEP 3

Once I had all the markings of the kitten in place, I then moved on to working up the darker shadows and fur texture. I mixed a more pigment-heavy solution using the black watercolour pan; again test your paint on a spare piece of paper before you start work on your drawing. I added darker defining shading around the eyes and pupils and used brisk flicking motions with the brush to describe the fur texture upon the body. I then gradually worked up the shadows around the face and paws. At this stage the drawing is really starting to take on a spark of life and movement.

STEP 4

Finally, I added some shading and texture to the toy and brushed in a subtle shadow beneath the hind paws of the kitten. The shadow gives the kitten a grounding, so that it no longer appears to be floating in space. Working up the detail of the toy ties the whole composition together and intensifies the kitten's expression of concentration.

Soft pastel techniques

Soft pastels can create beautifully atmospheric drawings and are great for suggesting soft textures like that of a cat's fur. They are made up of pure pigment held together with a gum binder. Pastels are easy to blend with either your finger or a tortillon, which means that you can create very subtle gradations of tone.

When working with pastels it is a good idea to use a paper with a texture that gives the pigment something to 'key' with, so that your marks remain in place. Once you have finished a pastel drawing you should use a spray fixative over the surface to prevent your picture from smudging.

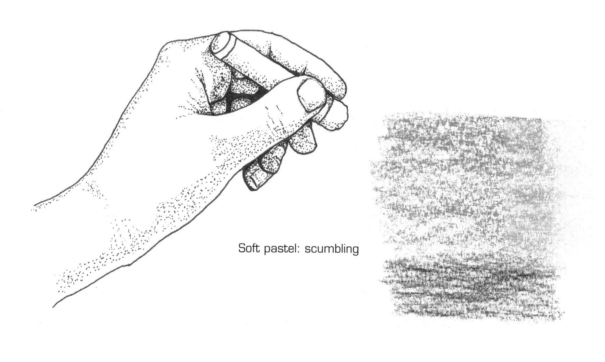

Soft pastel: scumbling

Soft pastel: blending

White cat resting: subtle tonal variation

With this project, I wanted to use the pastels to evoke the soft, silky texture of a cat's fur. I created this drawing from life and was lucky enough to have a very docile and sleepy subject who didn't move the whole time I was working. The subtle smoky shading that can be achieved with this medium was perfect for drawing the luxurious long fur of this cat.

Materials
- 160 gsm (98 lb) fine grain pastel paper
- HB pencil
- black, white and grey soft pastels
- tortillon
- fixative

STEP 1
Taking my HB pencil, I sketched in the outline of the sleeping cat. Although her eyes were closed while I was drawing, I chose to draw them open. I felt the open eyes could act as a focal point in the midst of the mass of fur, drawing the viewer in. I started to describe the long fur using broken lines, flicking randomly in different directions upon the surface of the cat's body.

STEP 2
Using the white pastel stick, I blocked in the entire body of the cat. I held the pastel stick on its side so that I could apply the pigment to the paper quickly and evenly. I then began to add some strategically placed shading upon the body with my grey pastel. These marks start to bring the form of the cat to life and also begin to evoke the texture of the long, wavy fur.

STEP 3

I used the black pastel to darken the eyes and details around the face. I then began to work on adding shadow beneath the cat's body. This further contributes to the solidity and substance of the cat, marking it as a real three-dimensional form reclining on the floor.

STEP 4

Finally, I used my finger to gently smooth the black pastel and gradate the shadow from the dark intensity around the lower perimeter of the body to a lighter tone. This creates an atmospheric, dark halo of shade around the cat, acting in perfect contrast to the soft lightness of its body. I wanted to keep the shading on the body very light and spare to maintain this clear contrast. I think it helps to give the drawing a peaceful air which perfectly evokes the content demeanour of the resting feline.

Oil pastel techniques

Like soft pastels, oil pastels are pure pigment held together with a binder, but instead of gum, a non-drying oil and wax binder are used. It is this that differentiates the two mediums. Oil pastels produce bold, clear lines and are not particularly easy to blend as they are not powdery like soft pastels. Instead they have a malleable, paint-like texture and can be built up in layers on the surface of the paper. By their very nature these pastels are oily, and so it is a good idea to use quite a robust paper when working with them. Papers made specifically for oil pastels are available, but they are not a necessity – just make sure that you use a paper with a weight of 300 gsm (140 lb) or more.

Oil pastel: blending

Oil pastel: scumbling/feathering

Oil pastel: scratching off

Black cat: bold, painterly technique

My aim here was to create an image that was free of intricate detail and more focused on tone. This was perfectly fulfilled by the bold opacity of the oil pastel. I chose as my subject a beautiful black furry cat. Black cats are normally quite hard to draw; they can appear simply as a pair of eyes if seen in dim light, so I made sure that my model stood in strong sunlight. The light reflects beautifully off the side of the cat and the shaded areas stand in dark opaque contrast to these highlighted areas. I wanted to work up the fur texture in the latter and the layering technique was perfect to build up the visual idea of fur tufts.

Materials
- 300 gsm (140 lb) fine grain paper
- HB pencil
- black, white and grey oil pastel sticks
- willow charcoal
- tortillon

STEP 1

I sketched in the outline of the cat with my pencil, using broken lines to plan the textured furry surface of the cat's body.

STEP 2

I rubbed the black pastel stick lightly over the surface of the paper, roughly blocking in the darkest areas of the body.

STEP 3

Taking the grey pastel, I used the same technique to fill in the remaining areas of the cat's body. I took the white pastel and dabbed in the irises of the eyes.

STEP 3

I used a tortillon to blend the black pastel to produce a more uniform dark opacity. I then began to blend the grey pastel around the face, softening the borders between the black and grey areas. I began to add grey pastel to differentiate the legs of the cat.

STEP 4

I blended the rest of the grey pastel with the tortillon, and once I had achieved an even covering over the whole drawing I started to layer up the pastels. I used a firm pressure to apply the pastels to the paper, using bold strokes following the direction of the cat's fur.

STEP 5

Using the white pastel, I started to add texture to my base layer of pastel. Again following the direction of the fur upon the body, I slowly began to build up the layers and the surface took on a tangible quality that suggests the long, soft fur of the cat. With brisk strokes, I added curved lines each side of the nose to describe the whiskers. I wanted to anchor the cat to the ground and present the drawing as a proper composition, so, finally, with a stick of willow charcoal I blocked in some shade beneath the cat's feet and used my finger to gently blend and soften the edges of the cast shadow.

Pen and ink techniques

A pen can be handled in very much the same way as a pencil, although the obvious difference is that once a pen line has been made it cannot be erased. When working with a pen I like to plan my drawing in pencil before committing to the permanence of ink. Pens are available in a variety of forms, from very fine-nibbed mapping pens which can be used to create beautiful fine detail, to thick markers and brush pens with which you can block in large areas of saturated tone. I have a collection of pens with nib widths ranging from 0.1 mm for very fine detail to 0.5 mm to create bolder lines.

When it comes to paper, you don't need anything specific – just make sure it is thick enough to avoid becoming saturated and wrinkled. It should also hold the ink so that it does not bleed through and lose the clarity of your lines.

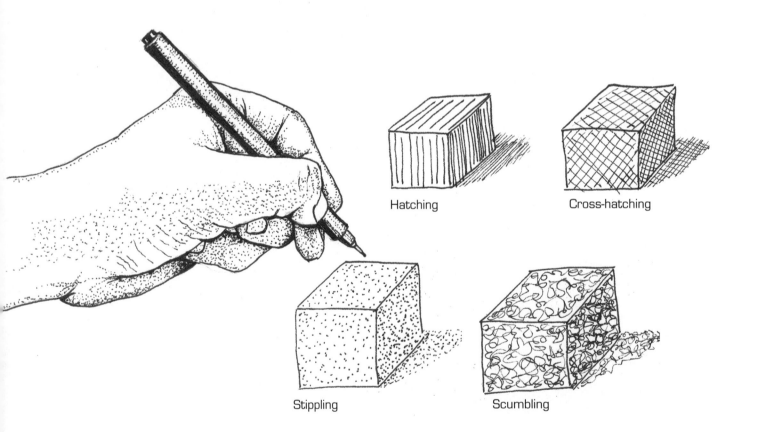

Hatching

Cross-hatching

Stippling

Scumbling

Cartoon cat: bold graphic style

To demonstrate the bold clarity that can be achieved with ink, I made this drawing slightly stylized. I worked from a photograph of a cat standing, looking out at the viewer. I wanted to simplify the image, ignoring the detail of texture and realistic shadow and concentrating purely on evoking character. To create a cheeky, loveable rogue of a cat, I added a slightly human quality to the facial features and expression.

Materials
- 160 gsm (98 lb) cartridge paper
- HB and 6B pencils
- 0.5 mm pen
- brush pen

STEP 1

I sketched in a very simplified outline of my cat using an HB pencil. To make the image bold and cartoon-like, when it came to strengthening my sketched lines I kept them very clear and unvaried; I added a few V-shaped breaks in the body contours to suggest the fur but kept this detail to a minimum. When drawing the face I departed completely from reality, adding a cheeky human smile.

STEP 2

Once I had established the form and expression of the cat I then began to work upon the pattern of the tabby markings with my pencil. Staying with the cartoon style I had developed while drawing the outlines, I started to sketch in stripes upon the body of the cat. I looked at how the markings in the reference photograph were positioned and then put in a simplified version on my drawing.

STEP 3

Next I went over my pencil lines with a 0.5 mm black pen. This really clarified the striped pattern.

STEP 4

Finally, using the brush pen, I inked in the stripes. I used a 6B pencil to add some very subtle fur texture to the white areas around the stripes and also lightly shaded the inside of the mouth and the irises of the eyes to set off the highlight and make the cat's expression sparkle. The final image has a clarity of contrast and form that fits perfectly with the cartoon style.

CHAPTER 5

CAT BREEDS

You have now learnt how to draw the shape of a generic cat, but physical characteristics vary greatly from one breed to another. In this chapter we shall explore how to draw some of the most popular breeds of cat, identifying what is particularly distinctive about the breed that makes it instantly recognizable. We shall examine the variety of fur markings which appear within a breed and study detailed portraits. By the end of the chapter you will be able to draw a range of cats, from fluffy and cuddly to sleek and slim.

Towards the end of the chapter we shall also look at how to draw the big cats; you will see how similar these wild cousins are to our familiar domestic moggy, and how with only a few simple tweaks you will be able to create beautiful portraits of lions and cheetahs.

The Siamese

The Siamese is one of the most popular and easily recognizable breeds of cat. It originated in Thailand (once known as Siam) and is characterized by its large almond-shaped eyes, triangular head, large ears and slender, muscular body. Siamese cats are also distinctive for their characteristic 'point' markings. These present as a pale fawn-coloured body and darker extremities – muzzle, paws, ears and tail. The varieties of Siamese markings are called seal point (the most common – fawn body and black face, ears, paws and tail), chocolate, blue, lilac, cinnamon, fawn, caramel, red, tortie, apricot and tabby point.

STEP 1

How to draw a Siamese face

The Siamese face is extremely distinctive and very easy to master once you have understood the basic shapes which can be used to construct the overall form. The following step-by-step examples show how to draw a Siamese portrait from the front and the side.

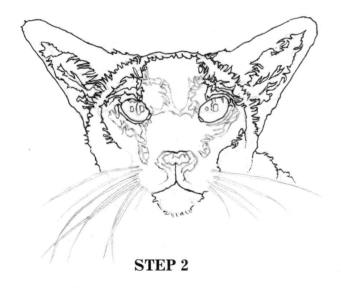

STEP 2

STEP 3

STEP 1

STEP 2

STEP 3

Siamese brothers dozing

Siamese cats are very affectionate and these two red tabby point boys Billy and Baby are inseparable. They like nothing better than snuggling up together and having a snooze! I wanted to show the languid, serene beauty of the breed and conjure the air of absolute peace and comfort in this drawing. I think their bed provides a perfect border to the composition and acts to contain and unify their joint poses. I used water-soluble pencil as it has an immediacy and subtlety of tone which perfectly captures the smooth silkiness of the cats' coats. This medium also has a large tonal range, from dark intensity to light transparent washes.

Materials:
- 300 gsm (140 lb) watercolour paper
- HB pencil
- HB and 8B water-soluble pencils
- size 4 round brush

STEP 1

I lightly sketched in the outlines of the cats and the bed using an HB pencil.

STEP 2

Using my HB water-soluble pencil, I began to locate the main areas of shadow upon the cats' bodies, rubbing the pencil lead softly over the paper to achieve a smooth, even coverage. I then began to lightly shade in the facial tabby point markings. I darkened the half-closed eyes; usually I would leave a little highlight to give a sparkle, but in this case I wanted to heighten the feeling of sleepiness so I made them shaded.

STEP 3

Taking the 8B water-soluble pencil, I shaded the bed behind the bodies of the cats. I used a firm pressure to create a dark, intense tone to set off the light, creamy luminosity of the cats' forms. I also used the 8B pencil to darken the eyes further. Taking my round brush moistened with a little water, I began to blend the HB shading to a smooth, subtle gradation.

STEP 4

Using my moistened brush again, I blended the 8B shading on the bed and the eyes. Then, with the dissolved pigment on my brush, I began to smooth in subtle texture on the cats' bodies to evoke the fur. Next, with my HB pencil, I drew in the ribbed stitching on the padded sides of the bed, curving and wrinkling it to evoke the soft fabric.

STEP 5

Finally, I used my 8B pencil to add some shading to the stitched lines of the bed and blended it out with a moist brush. This really clarifies the direction of light within the composition and helps to give a three-dimensional illusion to the drawing.

The Burmese

The Burmese breed originated in South East Asia. In the 1930s, one female was taken to the USA and bred with a Siamese. From then on the descendants of Burmese cats in the West were moulded into two different breed standards by American and European breeders. These standards differ mainly in respect of head and body shape – the European tends to be more Siamese-like, so has slender, long legs and body and a pointed, wedge-shaped head, large ears and almond-shaped eyes, while the American standard is a stockier cat with an overall 'roundness' to its appearance: its head, eyes and paws are all smoothly rounded and the muzzle is flattened. The legs are shorter than the European Burmese, giving the cat a compact, sleek physique. All Burmese cats have a very short, glossy coat of uniform colour.

How to draw a Burmese face

I have concentrated on the American standard of Burmese in the following drawings because they are so different from the Siamese. These two portraits really emphasize the roundness which clearly characterizes this standard of the breed. Both drawings were executed in water-soluble pencil, a medium which perfectly evokes the smooth glossiness of the Burmese coat. Follow these step-by-step examples and you will soon be able to master the Burmese portrait.

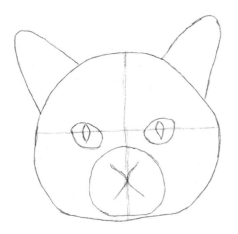

STEP 1

STEP 2

STEP 3

STEP 4

STEP 1

STEP 2

STEP 3

STEP 4

Burmese cat lying in his basket

Burmese cats are not your average, wild, independent feline; they hate being left alone for long periods of time and their main love in life is their human companion. I wanted to emphasize this loyal, loving nature in my drawing. The cat gazes out from the picture plane, making direct eye contact with the viewer; you can really feel the intensity of the cat's expression and this establishes a strong connection between the viewer and the drawing. I chose to execute the drawing in charcoal as the medium really conjures the smooth softness of the Burmese's beautiful coat.

Materials:
- HB pencil
- 160 gsm (98 lb) fine grain paper
- willow charcoal
- compressed charcoal pencil
- putty rubber
- tortillon
- fixative

STEP 1
Using a freshly sharpened compressed charcoal pencil, I sketched in the outline of the reclining Burmese cat. I sketched in some lines to roughly locate the top of the basket and the edges of the blanket which finishes beyond the cat's shoulder and beneath its rear end.

STEP 2
Holding the willow charcoal on its side, I gently rubbed it against the surface of the paper, blocking in a light tone to the whole area of the cat's body. I then blended the charcoal to an even finish with my finger.

STEP 3

With the compressed charcoal pencil I sketched in all the darkest tones on the cat, around the eyes and other facial features and on the outlines of the limbs. This shading also starts to evoke the texture of the fur and brings the three-dimensional form of the cat to life.

STEP 4

I then began to add highlights to the mid-grey base tone with a putty rubber, moulding it into a wedge shape so that I could sweep out highlights on the fur.

STEP 5

Finally I began to describe the blanket and wicker texture of the basket. I drew in an intertwined linear pattern upon the surface of the basket with the compressed charcoal pencil and made some soft tonal gradations upon the blanket to bring to life the soft texture and gentle undulations of the material upon which the cat lies.

The Maine Coon

The Maine Coon is one of the most popular cat breeds in the world. It gets its name from the American state of Maine, where the breed was first developed. The Maine Coon is well suited to the cold weather of this region, with its large, robust physique and long, thick, luxurious coat. It likes nothing more than being around people and is characterized as being very intelligent with a gentle but playful personality, a quality which has led people to refer to it as a 'dog-like cat'. The Maine Coon comes in a variety of colours, but it generally has a tabby-like appearance with blacks, browns and whites mingled together in the long, silky fur.

STEP 1

STEP 2

STEP 3

STEP 4

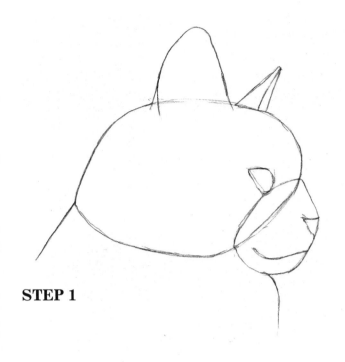

STEP 1

STEP 2

How to draw a Maine Coon head

The Maine Coon's most obvious characteristic is its long, wavy fur, which in male cats forms a full leonine mane around the neck. It also has distinctive ear tufts, giving a lynx-like appearance. In these portraits I wanted to capture the beauty of the Maine Coon's fur. The first was created using pen and ink and then a wash to establish the mid-tones. Make sure the ink pen you are using is waterproof if you want to introduce a wash to your drawing.

STEP 3

The Maine Coon sitting

The distinctive feature of the Maine Coon is clearly its long, wavy fur and it is this quality which I wanted to really show off in my drawing. I felt watercolour would be a great medium with which to evoke the gently curled locks of hair, as the paint is easily manipulated into smooth flowing strands. I chose to depict the cat in a sitting position to really allow the coat to be shown off in all its voluptuous beauty.

Materials:
- 300 gsm (140 lb) watercolour paper
- HB pencil
- black and Payne's grey watercolour paint
- size 4 round brush

STEP 1

Using an HB pencil, I began by laying out the general form of the seated cat with rounded, simplified shapes.

STEP 2

Once I was happy that I had an underlying physical structure that was proportionally correct, I began to add detail to the outline and mark out the areas of texture and tonal variation upon the surface of the cat's fur. I also added the detail of the facial features and flanked the muzzle with beautifully long whiskers!

STEP 3

I mixed a transparent solution of Payne's grey and slowly began to brush in a light tonal variation, using my pencil lines as a guide to help me place my brush strokes.

STEP 4

Using the black watercolour paint, I mixed a more pigment-heavy paint solution and used this for another tonal variation to darken the shaded recesses within the curly waves of the cat's coat.

The Bengal

The Bengal has a very distinctive coat pattern which looks like that of a jungle wild cat – the body is marked with dark stripes and spots which are highly contrasted against a tan base colour. The breed was developed by cross-breeding domestic cats with the Asian leopard cat, and this selective breeding eventually developed the characteristic coat pattern from which the Bengal is so easily recognized. The breed is generally larger than the average domestic cat, with a slender, muscular physique.

Bengal cats are playful and thrive on human attention. They are very active and have been known to spring to heights of more than 1.2 m (4 ft) from the ground. Unlike most felines, they love splashing about in water, a trait which may have been passed down through their wild cat ancestry.

STEP 1

STEP 2

STEP 3

STEP 4

How to draw a Bengal face

Much of the enchanting beauty of the Bengal's face comes from the perfect symmetry of its facial markings and the aloof, serene expression. I created the face here with pen and ink and used a stippling technique to suggest the characteristic markings. I used water-soluble pencil for the profile drawing; I added soft, light shading with the HB water-soluble pencil to the whole of the head to establish a mid-tone and then introduced the darker tones of the markings with the 8B pencil. The soft, fluid finish was achieved by gently blending the pencil with a wet round brush.

STEP 1

STEP 2

STEP 3

STEP 4

Bengal mother and kitten

I wanted to make the bold patterned markings of the Bengal the focus of this drawing. I also aimed to evoke the sleekness of the coat. I used soft pastel to create this piece, since it has a good tonal range and can be blended easily in order to suggest the soft quality of the cat's fur. I love this composition, with both mother and kitten boldly staring out from the picture plane, making unwavering eye contact with the viewer. This confident serenity perfectly sums up the Bengal's temperament.

Materials:
- 160 gsm (98 lb) fine grain pastel paper
- HB pencil
- black, white and grey soft pastels
- tortillon
- fixative

STEP 1

First I sketched in the outline of the two cats, using an HB pencil.

STEP 2

Taking my black soft pastel, I began to shade in the shapes of the Bengal's patterned coat and add detail to the faces. I used a firm pressure to apply the pastel to the paper to produce a dark, saturated tone which contrasted well with the white of the paper.

STEP 3

Using a firm pressure to apply the white soft pastel, I filled in the areas of bare paper around the dark areas of the cats' markings.

STEP 4

I then used the grey pastel to add texture and a mid-tone to the white areas. Finally, I added some shading beneath the pair with the black pastel and used the tortillon to blend the shadows to a smooth finish.

Big cats

Every cat owner knows that their seemingly docile domestic feline has a wild side! We do not need to look hard to see how small the separation is between the domestic cat and its feral cousins. Cats may have formed a close bond with human beings – to the feline advantage, of course – but they still retain their instinctive behaviours, most notably the desire to hunt. Observing your cat in the garden, transfixed by a bird or mouse, you can easily see that they have not forgotten their place in the natural world.

   The next two drawing projects focus on capturing the beauty of wild cats. You will notice that the basic forms that are used to construct the physique of the big cat are practically the same as those we have used to draw our domestic cats throughout the book so far.

Materials:
- 300 gsm (140 lb) cartridge paper
- HB pencil
- 0.3 mm and 0.5 mm pens
- HB water-soluble pencil
- size 4 round brush

Mother cheetah and cubs

The cheetah is famed for being the fastest land mammal and its anatomy reflects this remarkable ability to chase prey, with its slender muscular body, deep chest, small head and long thin legs. The most obvious distinctive feature of the cheetah is its spots and it is the beauty of this patterned coat that is the focus of my drawing. I used pen and ink to complete this drawing because I felt the intense tonal contrast between the ink and the paper would be the perfect way of showing off the cheetah's spots in all their beauty.

   Cheetahs have large litters of cubs and are very nurturing mothers. I also wanted to express this quality in my drawing; the mother stays alert and watchful, while her cubs can relax behind her, safe and secure.

STEP 1

I used an HB pencil to sketch in the outlines of the mother cheetah and her two cubs.

STEP 2

This stage might look painstaking but it really is worth it – after all, a cheetah just isn't a cheetah without its spots! So I slowly began to draw in the markings upon the coats with my pencil. Throughout the process I paid close attention to how each spot was positioned in relation to the others and with this methodical approach I was able to develop the three-dimensional form of the bodies as well as establish the characteristic pattern.

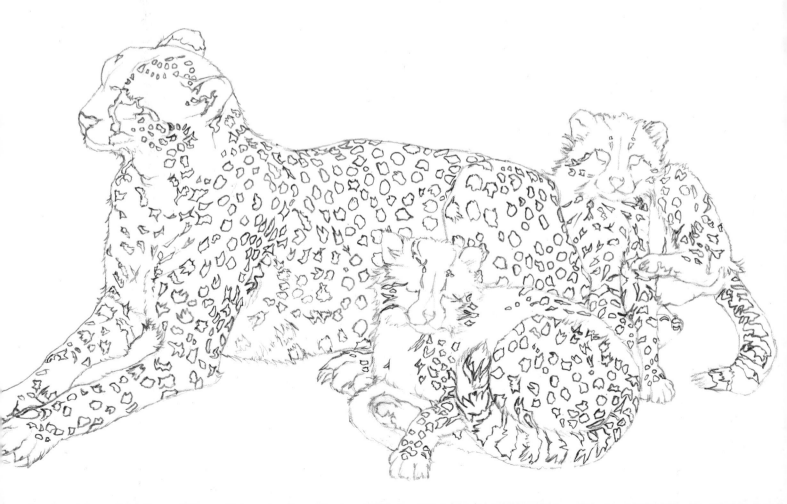

STEP 3

This is where careful planning pays off! Using a 0.5 mm cartridge pen, I began to shade in all the spots and the eyes of the cheetahs. This stage is relatively easy and when you have finished the results are quite dramatic, with the black inked areas contrasting starkly with the white paper to create a beautifully clear depiction of the cheetah's markings.

STEP 4

I then went over my outline in pen and added some areas of stippling to evoke a little texture and subtle shadow upon the cheetahs. Finally, with an HB water-soluble pencil, I added some light shading beneath the mother and her cubs and with a wet round brush I blended the shading to a subtle gradated finish. This final touch of shading fixes the trio upon the ground and gives them a physical context. If you are going to use a wash in an ink drawing, always remember to check that your ink is waterproof, otherwise you will risk blurring or entirely dissolving your inked workings.

Lion

The lion is the second largest of the big cats after the tiger and makes its home on the African plains. It is probably the most social of all the big cats and lives in family groups called 'prides' that use strength in numbers to take down their prey. The adult male lion is a highly distinctive, noble-looking beast with its chiselled face, huge mane and muscular body. It has been a symbol of strength and power for centuries and it is this nobility that I wanted to capture in my drawing.

Materials:

- 160 gsm (98 lb) fine grain paper
- HB pencil
- black, grey and white oil pastel sticks
- tortillon

STEP 1

I began by sketching out the form of the lion using an HB pencil.

STEP 2

I rubbed the grey pastel stick lightly over the surface of the paper, shading in the body, legs and tail of the lion to produce a scumbled, textured mid-tone. Using the grey pastel again, I added some rough line detail to the rear portion of the mane. This began to establish the thick furriness of the male lion's most characteristic feature.

STEP 3

I covered the face of the lion with white oil pastel, applying the stick to the paper with a firm pressure. Using the same pressure, I began to apply the white pastel to the scumbled grey shading that I had worked on in the previous step. This addition of white pastel to the grey blends and smooths the roughness of the previous shading application and produces a finish which perfectly emulates the lion's softly textured body fur. I took the grey pastel and applied it to the paper with a firmer pressure to add to the line texture of the mane. I then began on working up the facial detail of the lion using the black oil pastel, applying the stick to the perimeters of the eyes and the nose and mouth. I added some more darker shading to the top of the mane above the lion's ears. I also darkened the lower portion of mane where it meets the lion's body. I added some subtle black lines to define the shadow between the lion's rear and its tail.

STEP 4

I used this stage to blend the existing working and to add the all-important fur texture to the lion's mane. I added lines and textural detail to the grey part of the mane with black pastel and then used the white pastel to add subtle highlights. I applied the grey pastel to the front part of the mane and around the face, picking out shaded and texture detail upon the face. Next I smoothed the rear portion of the mane with a tortillon and added some subtle highlights with the white pastel.

STEP 5

In this final step I concentrated on defining the musculature of the lion's body by rubbing the point of my tortillon on to the black pastel and using the residue of pigment to smudge subtle shading on to the legs, ribcage, tail and outline of the lion. I then worked on establishing some detail on the rock upon which the lion stands, layering the grey pastel over the white and then finally adding some darker line detail with the black pastel.

CHAPTER 6

CAT COMPOSITIONS AND CATS IN ART

Cats are highly intelligent creatures and have adapted their behaviour over hundreds of years to take advantage of the comfort and safety that living with humans can bring. However, this domestication does not mean that they have lost all of their natural animal instincts; we can still observe our feline friends displaying similar behaviours to those we observe in the big cats filmed for wildlife documentaries. Whether snuggled up next to us on the sofa or prowling through the garden vegetation, cats provide us with endless visual stimulation that inspires us to stretch our skills by tackling new subjects.

In this chapter we shall explore how to create beautiful compositions, drawing the cat within its environment. We shall also look at how the cat has been depicted by artists throughout the ages by re-creating some of their most inspiring works. This exercise of studying and copying the work of others will help you to develop new visual approaches and ultimately pave the way for the evolution of your own unique and distinctive style.

Kittens among flowers

Kittens are well known for being playful and always on the go, until they flop down, exhausted, and fall into a deep sleep. As with any young animal, this play is the means by which a kitten learns how to fit in and adapt to its environment. In this drawing my aim was to create a harmonious composition where the primary subjects, the two kittens, are naturally framed by the surrounding flowers and foliage. They gaze intensely from the picture plane, drawing the viewer into the composition. The beauty of the two kittens is heightened by the floral border. I developed the composition by making sure the horizontal and vertical elements were balanced to produce an image that is a pleasure to view. I decided to create this image in watercolour because it allows you to achieve clear detail and also subtle gradation of tone.

Materials:
- 300 gsm (140 lb) watercolour paper
- HB pencil
- black and Payne's grey watercolour paints
- size 4 round brush

STEP 1

I began by planning the main vertical and horizontal elements of the composition as they will act as a basic framework upon which to develop the forms of the kittens within a setting that will show them off as the main focus of the image. This careful planning at an early stage ensures that the kittens will not get lost within their background.

STEP 2

Once I had established this very basic
structural framework, I began to sketch in
the more refined outline of the kittens and
drew the outlines of the flowers and leaves
surrounding them.

STEP 3

I mixed a dilute paint solution using Payne's grey and loosely brushed a subtle mid-tone on to the log in front of the kittens and on the petals of the flowers. I used the same paint mix to establish a texture upon the kittens' coats.

STEP 4

I used the black watercolour paint to mix a pigment-heavy solution and with this I began to paint in the darkest tones of the composition: the outlines of the kittens' facial features, the texture of the log and the patterns on the flower petals. Then I began to develop the finer details of the surrounding foliage.

STEP 5

I used this final stage to harmonize the two extremes of tonal contrast by adding tone and detail to the leaves in the foreground and adding fine brush strokes to the kittens' coats.

Cat sitting in a tree

Cats are expert climbers, so I couldn't resist creating a composition where a tree frames our feline subject. I wanted to use strong diagonals in the image to enclose the form of the cat, placing it in the very centre of the composition in the apex of the V-shape formed by the branches. I intended the image to be strong and bold, with much of the initial impact relying on tonal contrast, so I decided to create it using soft pastel and charcoal.

Materials:
- 160 gsm (98 lb) fine grain paper
- HB pencil
- willow charcoal
- black, white and grey soft pastels
- tortillon
- putty rubber
- fixative

STEP 1

I started planning the rough layout of the composition by lightly sketching in the diagonals of the tree branches with my HB pencil, then using these to help me sketch in the rough form of the cat, its body nestling snugly within the nook produced by the branch intersection.

STEP 2

I built up my refined outline upon this structural framework sketch. I developed the form of the cat and added lines denoting its markings. It has beautiful black and white patches on its coat, and it was these bold markings that first inspired the initial idea for the style of the drawing. I then drew in the leaves on the left-hand side of the composition. This detail acts as a border to the eye, preventing the viewer's attention from wandering away from the central focus of the image: the perching cat. Once I had added these leaves I took a critical look at the image and felt it was still missing something to balance the right side, so I added another vertical branch which acts as an equal opposite border to keep the eye focused on the centre of the composition.

STEP 3

I used this step to establish the darkest tone of the drawing: the black of the cat's fur. I rubbed the black pastel hard against the paper to produce an intense dark tone. I applied the white pastel to the rest of the cat, using the same method. I then turned my attention to the tree and rubbed charcoal softly over the surface area of the branches; I used willow charcoal because it is very soft and easy to blend, and is great for building up surface texture.

STEP 4

I used my finger to blend the willow charcoal on the tree to a smooth finish and then, with my putty rubber moulded into a chisel shape, erased curving lines into the surface to evoke the texture of the bark. Next, I added some textural detail to the white fur of the cat using the grey soft pastel, blending the marks out with the tortillon. I then used the excess pastel clinging to the tortillon to shade a mid-tone into the irises of the cat's eyes. With the black pastel, I began to darken the twigs on the right-hand side and added in the veined details upon the surface of the leaves.

STEP 5

With the black pastel, I darkened
the areas of bark around the lines
which I had erased into the willow
charcoal in the previous step. This
really starts to accentuate the
textural quality of the bark and
helps to bring the composition
together.

STEP 6

I used this final step to work on the detail of the leaves. I lightly shaded them with the willow charcoal and blended and lightened this shading with my finger. I then added some final subtle highlights to the foreground branch with the white pastel. As a final touch, I darkened the outline of the cat's chest. This helps the cat to stand out against the white paper of the background and makes the physical form more solid and tangible.

Cat asleep in its owner's lap

We treat our feline companions with the same care that we show to the human members of the family; they are always there to have a snuggle with when we're feeling down and they never answer back! Quite simply, they are the perfect companion. My main concern when planning this composition was to make sure I clearly evoked this connection between the cat and its owner. I felt the best way to do this was to use the hands and paws as a tangible physical link between the two. Eye contact is important within a drawing to convey mood and draw the viewer into an emotional engagement, and in this instance I used the lowered gaze of the woman as yet another link to connect the pair – the image sets up not only the physical but also the spiritual interaction between the cat and its owner. I wanted the whole atmosphere of the composition to be one of calm and peaceful relaxation and so chose to complete the drawing with very subtle tonal variation using a pencil.

Materials:
- 160 gsm (98 lb) fine grain paper
- HB, 4B and 8B pencils

STEP 1

I used this initial step to establish the key directional lines which would form the structure of the finished composition. With my HB pencil I sketched in the triangular shape which is set up by the position of the woman's arms and the raised paw of the cat. I made sure that the point where the paw and fingers touch was positioned near the centre of the page to make it clear that this interaction was a key feature of the image. I sketched in the outlines of the faces, making them almost in line, to again emphasize the closeness of the pair.

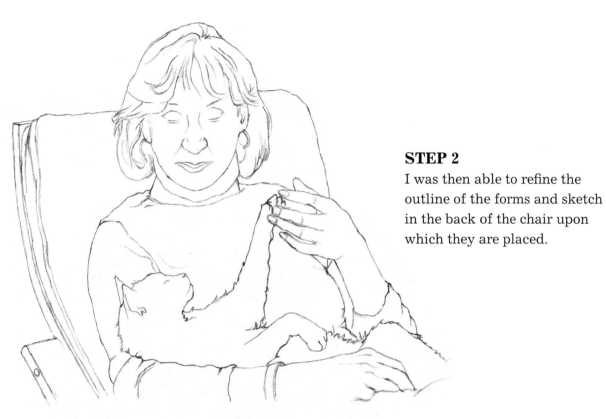

STEP 2

I was then able to refine the outline of the forms and sketch in the back of the chair upon which they are placed.

STEP 3

With the soft 4B pencil I began to lightly shade the surface of the woman's jumper so that the folds and wrinkles of the fabric became subtly visible. I used the same pencil to shade the arms, the contours of the woman's face and the texture of her hair. Her form now begins to take on a three-dimensional tangibility.

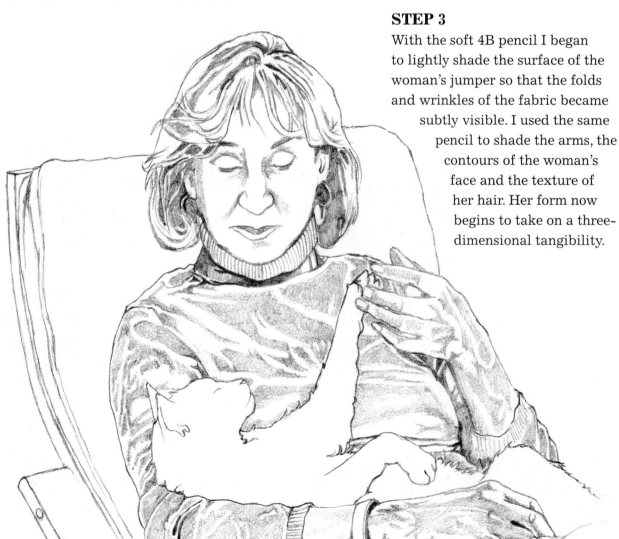

STEP 4

Next, I turned my attention to the detail of the cat lying within the woman's arms. I wanted to make the cat the darkest part of the drawing, so I worked up the shading and detail with the 8B pencil. With this darker tone established, I then realized that the woman's face needed more work to bring it up to the same level of detail as the cat and thus create greater unity within the image. I blended a soft midtone over the whole face and parts of the hair with my fingertip and then darkened the lowered eyelids with the 8B pencil.

STEP 5
I used this final step to work on the shading of the chair, again smudging in a subtle mid-tone with my finger and then working upon the variations in the creases of the fabric. Lastly, I softly darkened the inner side of the woman's hair. This final touch defines the perimeter of her face and makes it into more of a focal point within the composition.

Mother tiger carrying cub

There is no stronger bond than that between a mother and her young. In this drawing I wanted to bring to life the nurturing character of every female cat. Wild cats must be particularly committed to the rearing of their young, as there are so many dangers and threats to their survival. For this reason mothers must often carry their babies from place to place, and this drawing captures one of those moments.

I decided to depict the tiger in this image of motherly feline love. The distinctive striped coat and athletic muscular body make it one of the most beautiful members of the big cat family. I opted for pen and ink to establish a strong tonal contrast within the patterned coats, with subtle pencil shading and wash to create a background that would not detract from the boldness of the main feature of the composition – the tigers themselves.

Materials:
- 300 gsm (140 lb) cartridge paper
- HB pencil
- 0.3 mm pigment liner
- HB and 8B water-soluble pencils
- size 4 round brush

STEP 1

I began by sketching in the outlines of the mother tiger and her cub with an HB pencil. I then roughly laid out the rocky outcrops behind the pair.

STEP 2

This step is somewhat laborious, but all the hard work is worth it in the end! I sketched in the stripes on the tigers with an HB pencil, observing the overall pattern on the coats. I did not make my lines too regular, as I was trying to emulate the stripes as they appear on the three-dimensional form of the tigers' bodies – the curves of the stripes help to establish the solidity and shape of the forms. Note how the stripes are not evenly distributed on the mother tiger; they are densely spaced over her side and back legs and more sparse upon her foreleg. This variation of pattern is very common in the coats of wild cats.

STEP 3

All the groundwork laid down in the previous step paid off now! With the 0.3 mm pigment liner, I inked in my pencilled pattern. The transformation was quite radical and inspiring; the clear tonal contrast between the stripes and the white background has brought the drawing to life.

STEP 4

Now it was time to turn my attention to the background. I did not want the setting to draw focus away from the tigers so I took a subtle approach, using water-soluble pencil to lightly shade a texture into the rocky outcrops upon which the mother tiger steps. I used a gentle pressure with the HB water-soluble pencil so that the shading is translucent and smooth.

STEP 5

With a moistened round brush, I blended my shading so that the entire rocky surface acquired a light mid-tone which is distinctly darker than the white of the tigers' coats. This helps to project the cats into the foreground and makes them shine out of the picture plane. As a final touch, I added some deeper shading to the rocks with the 8B water-soluble pencil.

Cats in the history of art

Depictions of cats in paintings have often been symbolic, using the cat as a vehicle through which to express an idea. The cat has long been shown in paintings alongside a woman, both of them reflecting what were traditionally considered to be female qualities: elegant beauty, masking a wilful and infuriatingly independent character. This seductive combination has proved a popular subject for countless artists throughout the history of art.

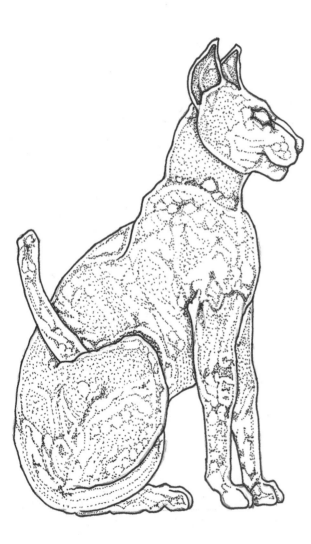

Cats in Ancient Egyptian art

Cats, known as Mau, were extremely important within Ancient Egypt and this is clearly reflected by the abundance of feline images which still exist in our museums and galleries. Cats were first domesticated for practical reasons – as natural hunters, they helped to control pests such as snakes and mice, so they were obviously very useful creatures to have around. On another level, the cat became a sacred symbol of fertility, to be worshipped, and they were often depicted in hieroglyphics and sculptural reliefs alongside women to represent protection and the nurturing qualities associated with motherhood.

I was inspired to draw this image of a cat after looking at a relief which had been sculpted into the side of a stone sarcophagus, dating from around 1000BC. The image is very stylized; no attempt is made to capture the three-dimensional form of the cat. Its charm lies in its simplification. It is definitely recognizable as a feline, and this is remarkable and beautiful to behold. The pared-down visual elements which we all associate with the feline form help to evoke the very essence of the cat. I completed the drawing in pen and ink, a medium which suits the simple boldness of this style perfectly.

Bacchiacca's *Woman with a Cat*

This portrait was made using oil paint on a wooden panel in the 1540s. There was a great tradition throughout the Renaissance for important people to commission portraits of themselves holding exotic accessories which would demonstrate to friends and acquaintances their wealth and status in society. This lady would definitely have been a woman of importance, partly because she was able to commission a portrait of herself in the first place, but also because of her exquisite silk gown upon which she cradles her pet. She stares thoughtfully into the distance, presenting the viewer with a three-quarter profile bearing a contemplative and peaceful expression.

Leonardo da Vinci sketches

Leonardo da Vinci, arguably the greatest artist of the High Renaissance, is said to have stated that 'even the smallest feline is a masterpiece'. From this we can deduce that the cat was a creature very much admired by this pioneering artist. His sketches of cats in many different positions, drawn in 1513, show how Leonardo made his drawings from meticulous observation of nature; the drawings are faithful re-creations of the feline form as we know it. There is very little of the stylization that we see in the work of Bacchiacca, whose art is very much rooted in the stylistic tradition of the Early Renaissance and still retains vestiges of the woodenness of the Gothic style. Leonardo was one of the first artists to take drawing and painting into a new style which is almost photographic in its realism.

Renoir's *Woman with a Cat*

Auguste Renoir was one of the leading pioneers in the development of the Impressionist movement, a style which expressed the simple beauty of the natural form using bold, free lines and loose brush work to produce an image with real visual immediacy and intensity. As a man whose inspiration came from nature, it is no surprise that Renoir included the cat in so many of his portrait compositions, depicting them in a lifelike and naturally beautiful style.

This portrait was painted in 1875, using oil on canvas. It depicts a beautiful young woman clasping a tabby cat to her chest. Her eyes are downcast and her expression conveys an air of the simple contentment with which every cat owner will be familiar – the warm feeling experienced when having a cuddle with a beloved pet. The composition is simple but extremely compelling: the woman's arms enfold the cat and her right hand is buried in its fur, helping to heighten the soft warmth of the embrace.

Materials:
- 160 gsm (98 lb) fine grain paper
- HB pencil
- black, white and grey oil pastels
- tortillon

STEP 1

Renoir's style tends towards a soft, rounded approach to form, so I accentuated this when I began sketching in the outlines of the woman and the cat. I held my pencil loosely and applied it lightly to the paper to create a subtle outline. I could strengthen this later once I was totally happy with the forms and how they interacted within the overall composition.

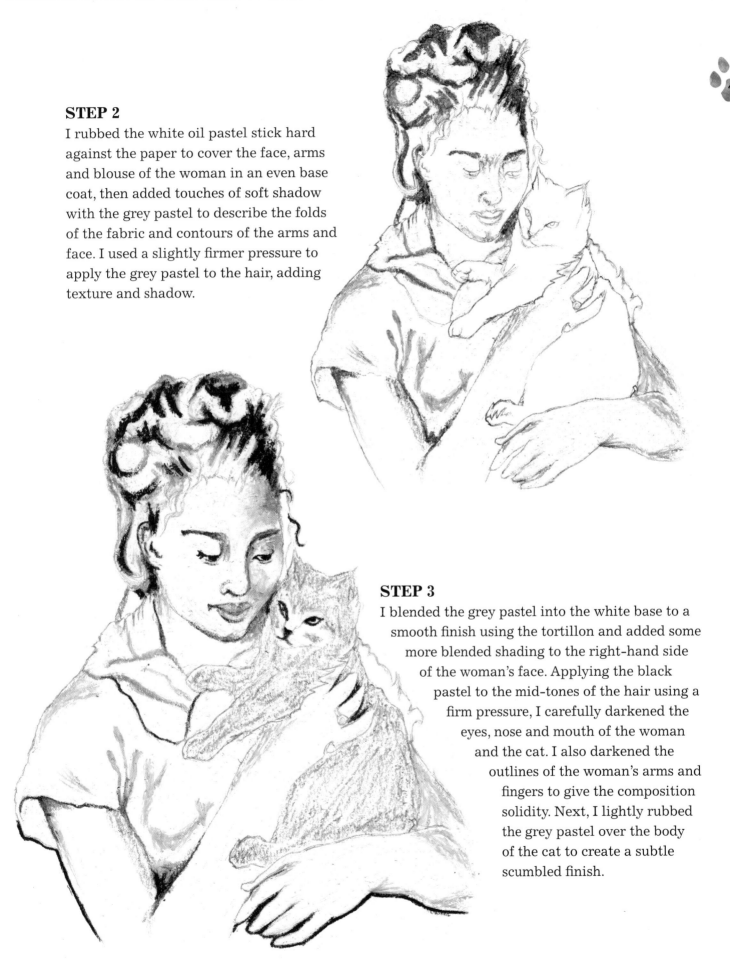

STEP 2

I rubbed the white oil pastel stick hard against the paper to cover the face, arms and blouse of the woman in an even base coat, then added touches of soft shadow with the grey pastel to describe the folds of the fabric and contours of the arms and face. I used a slightly firmer pressure to apply the grey pastel to the hair, adding texture and shadow.

STEP 3

I blended the grey pastel into the white base to a smooth finish using the tortillon and added some more blended shading to the right-hand side of the woman's face. Applying the black pastel to the mid-tones of the hair using a firm pressure, I carefully darkened the eyes, nose and mouth of the woman and the cat. I also darkened the outlines of the woman's arms and fingers to give the composition solidity. Next, I lightly rubbed the grey pastel over the body of the cat to create a subtle scumbled finish.

STEP 4
Looking closely at my reference image,
I emulated the shapes and spacing of the
tabby stripes using the black oil pastel.
Then I darkened the outline of the top
of the woman's hair.

STEP 5
Finally, I added some more shadow to the woman's hair and left arm. This final shading brings the image together and adds cohesion between the two, with the cat held in a loving embrace.

Index